DESECRATION OF THE BLACK MAN

THE VICIOUS CYCLE

An

Empress

Makeda Gordon

&

Ras Jah Strength

Collaboration

Desecration of the Black Man

The Vicious Cycle

Copyright © 2017 by Solomon & Makeda Publishing

All Rights Reserved. No Parts of this book may be reproduced in any form without the express written consent of Publisher/Author, except in the case of brief quotations embodied within relevant articles and book reviews for print and electronic media.

Foreword

A Desecration is a violating of the sanctity (that which is set apart, purified, or made productive), a profaning; or to treat disrespectfully, irreverently, or outrageously. The "Desecration of The Black Man" is the violation of the sanctity, to profane; or to treat disrespectfully, irreverently, or outrageously, the genetic caretaker, spiritual firstborn, and protector/provider of all creation. To completely know what this "Desecration" is, a reverse engineering is necessary; in order to discover the root cause of a machination that is as systematically elaborate as this.

First, let's be clear that a desecration of any type or kind is to remove the reverence, influence, strength, and/or power, that can or may be seen in that object or person. To be absolutely clear, "The Desecration of The Black Man" was and is to remove the reverence, power, influence, protection, leadership, guidance and salient being, from the minds and hearts of those most in need, and dependent, of such a man.

As a concept, the Desecration of The Black Man is a Desecration of the Black People. It is the "Thievery" and "Usurping" of a people's society and civilization building. This "Grand Scheme" and "Machiavellian Machination" is a "Hydra of Destruction"; creating the schizophrenia of an entire society of people, especially in the targeted group. No one is excluded from some accountability in its continuation, although some roles have an immense, intense, and critical effect; like that of the Black Woman.

When a study is made of the African descendants residing in the Americas, specifically the descendants of slaves, and especially in the United States of America, curious cancerous manipulations are found affecting them. Pigmentocracy is the most obvious and well known, regionocracy and religiocracy are some supporting pillars. But, the strongest desecration, that leads to depredation, is done from the "Badges and Incidents of Slavery", implemented by the "Jim Crow's Disorder" of "Gender Opposition".

Emptiness and Void, confusion and disobliging of the union, the family, the community, and the nation, becomes the reality of this particular version of our Post-Traumatic Jim Crow Syndrome Disorder. There is no worthiness believed, no value perceived, no accountability of adding to the betterment and upliftment of our people. An aimless walk through life, with no equity capital earned for future generations, has become the habitual nature of this ancient species; and there seems to be no change happening in the near future, because he is embattled with his helpmeet

III

For the "Desecrated Black Man", she has become a treacherous and degenerate, manufactured character, whose learnings, ways, and scheming has destroyed the union of "Black Identity". Whose licentious ways inspired, by their very profligacy, a gender war. This now putrid union is at a reprobate degree, and has created a dissolute people; driven only by indecorous copulations.

The fictional and fractal interactions of their non-coalescing ideas and understandings are the bricks and mortar between them. Thoroughly baked by the unrelenting heat of unresolved, un-healing, anger, pain, and suffering, here in the West. These bricks and mortar became living barriers against any unity building, equanimity, or harmony, of our collective. As is said in the infamous Willie Lynch Letter "Distrust is stronger than Trust". So, in this frozen psychological state of independence, for the Black Woman; but a mentally weak and dependent, spiritually broken, but physically strong, state of the Black Man, We Lost Everything!

In the hierarchy of needs, each level has a suitable knower-giver/receiver-learner process. Meaning, one gender is better suited to know and give, while the other is better positioned to receive and learn. Knowing this should allow the Black Identity, Black Union, to resolve its leadership and role issues that plague it. We must begin to establish the better abled and better suited, of

IV

the male and female, in leading the way in solving the myriad of problems we now face.

Multiple generations of louche empowerment have marked the heart and attitude of the Black Identity, and reclassified it as the "World's Demimonde". Black Identity is seen as a hetaera if a certain appearance criterion is met, but a doxy if not. This has ruined Black Potential and created an ignominious psychosis.

A further assault is made through the social-economical influence of hedonism. Black social-economic exchange and comfort has been made into a pendulum between the genders and generations. The oscillation of this is done between the salacious lasciviousness of one and the munificent spendthrift of the other. A "Pleasure Principle" is the dominating force and influence.

There was an age when Black Identity had two forms of solidarity that emitted from our Oneness. They were based on different sources, but always continued the complementariness of the people. One form was a "Mechanical Solidarity", which comes from likeness, and is at its maximum influence when the collective conscience completely envelops our whole consciousness and coincides in all points with it. Mechanical Solidarity occurred when there wasn't too

V

much division of labor. Our societies were relatively homogenous because men and women engaged in similar tasks and daily activities. We had similar experiences and distinct institutions that expressed similar values and norms and tended to reinforce one another.

The norms, values, and beliefs we shared then were homogenous and confronted the individual with such overwhelming and consistent force, that there was little opportunity for selfish individuality or deviance from our collective conscience. Traditionally, our culture experienced a high level of social and moral integration, there was little individuation, and most behaviors were governed by social norms which were completely embodied in our religion.

Now the second type of solidarity is called "Organic Solidarity", and it is that which develops as a by-product of the continued divisions of our labor. When we became part of a more complex society, individuals played more specialized roles and became ever more dissimilar in our social experiences, material interests, values, and beliefs. Individuals in our so-called advanced sociocultural systems had less in common; however, they did become more dependent on each other for a unique survival. For example, as a Black-Smith I don't grow my own food, and as a Farmer, you don't iron work.

VI

The growth of individualism was an inevitable result of the increased division of labor. This individualism though can only develop at the expense of the common values, morality, beliefs, and normative rules we share. With the loosening of our common rules and values, we lost our sense of union, community, and identity. Our social bonds were thereby weakened, and our social values and beliefs no longer provided us with coherent or insistent moral guidance.

Now Europeans, and especially European-descended Americans, lack the complete mastery of self, in any systematic, organized, or religious/spiritual way, in their history, to assist Us in any capacity, except the one category of self-destruction, which they have mastered. They lack the complex and abstract spectrum of processes that the Black Mind readily use for even the most minute of operations and applications. The European, and his descendants, are themselves remote derivatives of the Black Man. But they are retrograded, and are without the conscious awareness of the self-soul-spirit. The European descendants are genetically, cognitively, flawed in that the processes on the microscopic, cellular, and sub-atomic levels, do not have the connectivity and harmonics that are ever present in the Black Mind. Therefore, any science of Self, Soul, Identity Healing, that has come from them, cannot and

VII

will not be able to work, or succeed, towards correcting or healing the Black Mind or the Black People. Because first, we aren't just Black People, and secondly, it will take a system that has 180-degree reversal of our syndrome condition, with a 360-degree changeability that's catergoricaly detailed.

...Ras Jah Strength

Introduction

Most of the men that I know really don't consider themselves to be complexed at all, by definition. Most think of themselves as being very straight forward and obvious. I previously was one of those men. But after pondering, and contemplating, certain aspects of my past, and considering some circumstances of my present, I realized that there is more to me than meets the eye. And, that there is more to other men than what meets their eyes and understanding.

The realization of the "more of me than meets the eye" perception was a "wow" moment for me. I pondered how so much of who I am could go unnoticed, even by me, and it was shocking. But then, that gave me deep clarity as to some perplexing and confusing moments in my life. I finally got a look at the "Real Me", the "Complete Me". I know that this may seem like the "Confessions of a Bipolar", but if this is definitively true, and it is, then we are all bipolar, or tripolar, or however multiple-polars one can identify in the seeking to know thyself.

We all have complexities and degrees. It is just that women, for the most part, most of the time, express and admit to theirs, while men, for the most part, are denied theirs or express them grievously less; that's an open secret of the genders. No one really attempts to see a Layered man. No one attempts to understand the multiple deficiencies of the man until something goes wrong or someone is hurt. No one wants to really see men in vunerable or confused states. If they do, they blast out the rhetoric; Get it together, tighten up, loosen up, or some other saying that speaks light-hearted and nonchalantly about a serious issue in men.

So how do we know more, or realize more of ourselves? Well, divination could help. The concept of Enoptromancy, or divination by means of a mirror, an ancient science only spoken of in whispers, in the smallest of circles, among the most zealous of men, would be an excellent evaluation skill for men to use in a self-help, self-correcting, self-bettering manner. But, there is no guarantee that mastery of Enoptromancy would prevent an increase of the Pseudo-Self, or fuel a nascency of change. Therefore, a true "checks & balances" approach and execution must be utilized for optimal effect, drive, constancy, and efficiency. Let's not continue a sort of walking oneiromancy, or guessing profusely, with our lives. Wake Up and Realize!

You see family, time is not benevolent to the stringent unforgiving course that we are maintaining; as if we are unaware of the fiascoes that have preceded this reckoning point that we are now intimate with. Time has its own purpose for each individual, and it is to be determined by each one of us as to what that purpose is, and how to perform it as an autodidactive maven.

We have been on, and continue to be, a Self-Destructive course of Mayhem that is also destroying the lives of those who we say that we love; that are in proximity to us. On a grander scale, we are corrupting the society that we are a part of by being Non-Active, Dormant, Inert, and even Effeminate in carrying out the True Moral Values of Manhood. What men feel in and of themselves, and what society expects in and of them, does not lend a diagnosis to a man that something is wrong. Men usually don't find out that they have a problem, that they are a problem, that they stand in the way of progress, elevation, and betterment, until "All Hell" has broken loose.

Who am I? To most men, obliteration has caused in us the state where we would never ask that question of Ourselves. We don't ask who am I, and we definitely don't want to really know what state we are truly in. We believe who we are based on "what" we say we are, and that's that. The problem with this is that we do not consider if what we are saying is true, and if we should even be considering Ourselves in that way. In other words, we do not analyze, nor are we able to prove, if what we say that we are is the most productive; and is of the highest potential that we have, within us, to offer.

If we give any thought to this question we would discover that most times, we are referring to Ourselves as adjectives, and not Beings. Dressing up in adjectives can only cover the Truth for so long. In a matter of time, the conditions that underlay our troubled self, the cause of our suffering, will reveal themselves to us, and to the world around us; The Day of Reckoning is at hand.

So what shall we reckon? Well, the three basic, fundamental, and essential components of our existence are Flesh, Spirit, and Soul. They make up who we are. They are interconnected and interdependent. And depending on what we are doing, and where we are in life, one of them takes on a dominant role, and positions itself as a ruler over the others. If we have no knowledge or wisdom of how our Triune Being operates, nor understanding of the proper order and structure of it, we will be in a subjugation, through ignorant allowance, and the pain of it will become normality for us. When that happens, not if, we become the owners, managers, and distributors of that pain to the myriad of areas in our lives. Deluging, specifically, those areas that are occupied by those we claim to Love.

XII

Now, how do we fix the problems with ourselves that we do not even want to acknowledge? "By Being Still"! When we find that moment of stillness, so much will be revealed about ourselves, exposing the difference between what is True and Real and what is false and illusionary. We must put in some work, with true effort, to learn about the influences and effects that are concretizing as we Live. Each influence is playing some role that we must identify, analyze the intent of, and then make all of the corrections and adjustments that are necessary for the optimal betterment of ourselves. The knowing of Thy Self is the solvent for that concretizing that is leading us to becoming degenerate louches.

We cannot, and should not, allow a multiple licentious, wanton and profligate, existence to be in us or continue in us. We must think deeply, know higher, and understand more about our Triune Being so that we bring order and balance to Our Life. Harmony is the key that unlocks the peace and serenity that we were made to possess, manage, and distribute. And, there are two places that we need to better overstand so that harmony can be gained, the Spirit and the Flesh.

The spirit is a most wonderful part of the human being. Incorruptible, True, Distinguished, and Honorable, the Spirit's purpose is "Absolutely Divine". It urges towards betterment and elevation. It keeps its place as a beacon of light to those who may fall victim to darkness and loss within the soul. It reaches outwardly to what is cleansing and purifying; a help in any time of need.

The word Spirit is from the Latin spirare, which means "to breathe". It is that part of man that is immaterial. It can be labeled soul, personality, life force, will, consciousness, feeling, thoughts, and true existence.

In the Bible, Spirit occurs more than five hundred times. All of its use in the Biblical examples leave distinctive marks of indefinability. In Hebrew, it is found common to the word Ruach, and in the Greek, it is called pneuma. Both of these basically mean breath, wind, or Life force.

The Spirit can be associated with the Life Force that originated with God, a breath breathed into humanity by the creator.

From Spirit we get Spirituality, which is the condition of Spirit-Mindfulness, or devotion to God and the things of the Spirit. Spirituality is why we have practices like chastity, volunteering, ministry, monasticism, and evangelism.

Spirituality is where one's thoughts, beliefs, and religion becomes a daily part of their lives. The formation of spirituality comes from the unknown depth of existence and couples with our moral values.

The Spirit is a life-principle, comprehensive to a child of 7-11 years old. At this point, it begins to mean something to us. It is the rightness in deciding. It is the do, or not do, that we consider before an act, It even helps in believing or not believing. We do not make decision absent the Spirit. The Spiritual nature of man is the invisible cause and controlling the power of his visible material personality.

Since we have three universal centers, the one higher, the one lower, and the link uniting them. We need to overstand more about this link, in order to always function on the higher. The Spirit carries out the duties necessary for the higher self, but most of us over-rule it and carry out a different path that operates in the lower self.

The key to understanding why spiritual growth has not taken place, even if there has been a successful replacement of negative behavior, is due to the fact that we have not become "Awakened". To become "Awakened" we will need the changes in our behavior to be credited towards spiritual growth, and that means that we have to do the work ourselves. So long as we have a minister, pastor, preacher, teacher, messenger, or Messiah, we will be absent of "True Spirit" and our spiritual potential. The information that we've obtained has to cease being knowledge and begin being overstanding and wisdom. Wisdom will be the application, of knowledge and overstanding; and how it operates in our lives while affecting others. This we must do before we can begin to address how all of this manifest into flesh (body, world, environment, space, state, etc.).

Our flesh, what a complex and often misunderstood, misused, and abused gift from Our Greater Source. It is the instrument of Our connectivity to this World, and beyond. We need to know exactly what Our flesh is. But before We begin to discuss Our flesh in a purely subjective manner, let's point out its categorical representations that are relevant to this discussion. In needing to know exactly what Our flesh is we shall start with its compositional facts, and then move to Our basic philosophical origins. In this way, a foundation of information and knowledge is gained for further elaboration.

Our compositional make-up is of six (6) main elements. Why do We need to know this? Well, knowing Our compositional elements will heighten Our identification with the World Around Us. The more that We know about Ourselves, the more that We will relate to, and feel a sense of connectivity to, in Our everyday Lives. Here is Our compositional make-up: Carbon 18%,

XVI

Hydrogen 9.7%, Nitrogen 3%, Oxygen 65%, (mostly because of Our water content), Phosphorus 1%, Sulfur .27%, and about 3 of Trace Elements, which We contain in very minute quantities. Know also that, our compositional elements can be located in several different products found at Our local home/hardware stores. For example: Carbon-charcoal; Hydrogen and Oxygen-water; Nitrogen-fertilizer; Phosphorus-matches; and Sulfur-rubber. Look at how amazing life is. See how True Our "Being One with the World" is really backed by facts? Therefore, we have to look at Ourselves differently. We have to know ourselves in ways not taught anywhere but are Absolute Truths. If, and when, we do this, Life itself will change for Us. Life itself will change to Us. But let's not stop there, let Us re-discover Our philosophical origin.

Just so you know, Our Ancestors first identification of something called flesh was defined as "body" which to Us is known as a "corpse". In other words, only something dead was considered a body or flesh. While Life was present, that designation was never satisfactory; nor used. Living made the flesh more than it was capable of being, when defined by words.

An elementary place to discover the philosophical origin of flesh is in the Greek word sarx. Sarx describes the muscular part of the body. It is supposedly developed out of the four elements. Plato thought of flesh as rising out of blood, while Aristotle thought of its origin as stemming from moisture and theorized that thick blood arises out of flesh. The use of sarx broadens out to include the whole body, especially the physical body, which may be young, aging, or dead, the inner part of the skin, dried-up flesh, flesh of fruits, and even for the swelling in flesh.

Sarx is finally described as the Seat of Emotions. Stimuli affect the sarx, e.g. heat or cold, fear or pity, joy and pleasure. Desires are strictly attributed to sarx. Choices may be made, but in choices, there is a heed to the summons of nature that sarx is receptive to. Sarx is the seat of sorrow, too, but pleasure surpasses sorrow, hence Our propensity for addictions. Sarx expressed human lowliness and corruptibility in distinction from the Creator. In some references, Sarx relates closely to sin and pride.

Sarx, the flesh, is sometimes neutral but also denotes human creatureliness. This is bound up with sinfulness and ignorance, but it does not itself stand in contrast to the spirit; instead, it is the battleground of the conflict between the spirit of evil and the spirit of righteousness.

The flesh, in its philosophical origin in sarx, denotes humanity in its inability to know God. It is described to have a weakness in perception, that it has inner

XVIII

anxieties, and can only acknowledge a wisdom according to the categories of the world. It is what is defined as the part not able to inherit the kingdom without transformation. There is the suggestion that the flesh is vulnerable to temptation as well as corruption.

As the philosophical discussion continued into the Fourth and Third Centuries, the use of sarx was replaced by soma. Soma was then defined as the physical existence that ends with death. As such, it is distinct from the spirit and soul, without which it has no value. Physical existence is often felt to be an alien affliction, the sema (tomb) of the soul, the fetter that fate has ordained for humanity.

This view of soma (body) as the physically present person, with some stress on corporeality, has come down to us basically unchanged. The perspective of the body being associated with activity and suffering is the foundation of three major religions. That is why We needed to point out its actuality before going on further in Our discussion.

Our race, body types, how we think, and Our belief systems are ideals that we attribute to Our corporeality (Our relationship to how we experience). We can understand differently within each one of these areas of

XIX

Ourselves, anytime; given sufficient information, effort, and the aide of other people, if possible; from their experiences, knowledge, and resources.

    The flesh, body, or sarx houses Our Soul, which is a reservoir for what happens to us, and how we experience it in this world. Us men are so fortified in Our flesh, stamping Our Souls, 'til We begin to earn interest, compound interest, on the pain and suffering that We encounter in Our Living, from childhood to adulthood. With this innate ability, it's no wonder that the reference "Grumpy Ole Man" is used as a description of Our elder years, and has become sort of a fate for the majority of Us. Having a natural ability to harness pain was supposed to allow Us to maintain an even keel, not harness the pain, sufferings, trials and tribulations as part of Ourselves, and then begin to transpose them into a fuel, an energy, or identity. Doing that would be "Perpetual Pernicious Egoism," a complex idea coined for the purpose of creating a re-evaluating of the concept and system of Self-destruction.

    Man's folly is infinite, therefore, there must be an upgrade, elevation, and/or increase in the correcting ability of those who can analyze, recognize, and realize, his folly. Perpetual Pernicious Egoism (P.P.E.), the state that creates the unknown self, corrupt behavior, destructive attitude, obscene thinking, and vulgar desire, is an excellent description, or theory, of what

XX

categorically is wrong with Us. Any attempt to overstand P.P.E. would explain the evolutionary nature of wrongdoing, and how it applies to the mind and its activities in this manifested world.

    Defined as a state, P.P.E., once triggered into activity, constantly, and increasingly, produces harm and injury to the host, and its relatives. P.P.E. assumes that there is a benefit to the host in this state, in an increased continuance. It is a very difficult condition to break free and reverse from. It is also nearly an impossible state to be liberated from, without the identification of it. But that's just the nascent, once identified there must be a search for the resources, skills, or myriad of self-help assistances, to suppress and then remove any particular element of P.P.E. 's identified ailment; and then eventually P.P.E. itself in totality. We must consider the areas of science and religion to produce a coalescing panacea since P.P.E. has indicators that are categorically scientific and/or religious.

    Now P.P.E. is Our State, but from where did we gain it? Well, it's Our World Inheritance. This is the First Gift we receive that is tailor made, custom fitted for each of Us. No two P. P. E. are exactly the same, but no two P. P. E. are totally different. We all possess the qualities and characteristics of P.P.E. We just have different percentages, quantities, and mixtures. For example; one may have a quantity of anger with a certain percentage of abandonment issues, while another has a quantity of anger, with a mixture of low self-esteem, with a percentage of abandonment issues.

From the outside, those two examples could look so much alike, but, due to the mix of low self-esteem with anger, there will be other symptoms that reveal some hidden truths that need addressing. That's why a system of critical self-analyzation and investigative introspection will be required; before anyone of Us can be assured that We are maintaining a balanced, healthy, physical state.

The flesh, or body, or the physical, will have to be tamed, and/or domesticated, in order for Us to be well-functioning people. We have to learn, unlearn, and re-learn all that there is to Us, becoming productive, and change Our course towards being supplementary to that in which we are right now. This supplementary effort will produce the 180-degree healthy alternative to Our mire, and remove Us from propagating P.P.E. and its proven destructive nature in Us. We have to re-program those characteristics, values, and perspectives that the soul acknowledges in Our lower selves. We have to evaluate whether or not those pains or pleasures are applicable & healthy for Us, and we have to do that "Now"; or else the flesh will continue to damage Us; all the way to Our souls.

XXII

A major step in correcting Our State is to turn the clock back to the farthest point in Our memory, and hopefully, that is early childhood. In doing this, we are scrubbing those old wounds clean, applying the healing ointment of maturity, bandaging and beginning the healing process. Objective Observation is mandatory. Weigh the status of those circumstances, situations, issues, and environments we've experienced! Analyze the Truth in them that allows growth, and execute anything that stagnates.

For Us men, a positive or negative self-esteem, because of Our appearance, is not readily known. Yes, there is a percentage of men who for the most part narcissistically focus on their physical appearances. But for certain, the majority of Us are who We say that We are to Ourselves, within Ourselves. Whatever that deeply seeded ideal is, We take hold of it, ingest it, and then spew it into Our corporeality. We then affect the lives of all who come within Our "Sphere of Influence."

Our lives, as men, aren't supposed to be a shared consequence that We enjoin on others simply because We have lost Our "even keel" ability. Our lives are supposed to be testaments and lessons for those who could reap the benefit of Our experiences.

What We men do in conjuring an internal concept, and then expressing it externally, so that critical acclaim is perpetuated as Our identity, is different than the

XXIII

woman and her receptivity of the external, only to internalize it, and form her identity. It is a different procedure and process that is dealt with through different mechanics and operations.

    The moment has come for all of us to Self-Inspect, Self-Introspect, and Self-Correct. From that, we will design and activate the Higher Better Moral Values that lay dormant in Us. We always look at higher abilities as the tools for the changing of ways and behaviors in others; rarely do we feel that those same abilities, those tools, can be used, and should be used, in the changing of ways and behaviors in Ourselves. Welcome to the "Desecration of the Black Man".

…Ras Jah Strength

TABLE OF CONTENTS

Foreword: I

Introduction: VIII

Chapter One: .... **Daddy's Girl** 1

Chapter Two: .... **Sibling Rivalry** 12

Chapter Three: .... **Mother, May I** 23

Chapter Four: .... **The "*Easy*" Life** 31

Chapter Five: ... **The "Doll House" Syndrome** 41

Chapter Six: .... **Who is Jezebel** 52

Chapter Seven: .... **Introducing Mr. & Mr(s)** ... 67

Epilogue 75

Desecration of the Black Man
Empress Makeda Gordon

Daddy's Girl

Chapter One

What a beautiful notion it is to be a Daddy's Girl. Some of us have it, while others dream of it. Some say it's the first "boyfriend" a girl can have. After all, Daddy is the first male a little girl gets to be close to.

The idealistic version of the Father-Daughter relationship would be that he spoils her rotten. Not many Daddy's have the ability to say NO to his baby girl. When she is born, he spends all of his free time holding her and kissing her until she falls asleep on his chest. As she becomes a toddler and is driving Mommy crazy getting into everything, he becomes her Protector, her Fortress. He hides her behind his back and makes every excuse that he can for her just so that she will not get into trouble. Daddy can't stand to hear his Princess cry.

As she becomes school age, his protective nature morphs into over protection. He is so uncomfortable to leave her with strangers all day, even though they are only teachers. So he finds reasons to be there with her; he attends as many class

Desecration of the Black Man
Empress Makeda Gordon

trips as he can, volunteers to help out in class, and even throws her class parties for her birthday in addition to the outlandishly overdone themed party she begged for according to that year's "in" television show. Anything for his little girl.

Once the teen years come his level of protection has completed its metamorphosis into full "Beast Mode".

At this stage, she is beginning to pull away a little, hide some things from him, get closer to mom, notice boys; but, the worst of it all is PUBERTY. Daddy's baby girl has breast and thighs and her buttocks are firming from all of the sports he's had her in since she was five years old.

This is where the relationship becomes a bit murky. Now, Daddy and Daughter are not seeing eye to eye anymore. She wants freedom and he is busy building a prison so she can never leave the house again.

This Prison is painted in her favorite colors, has a big screen television, a stereo system with all the trimmings, not to mention her computer, Ipad and whatever the latest cellular phone is. He also keeps her stylishly dressed and her hair and nails are always on point. All she has to say is daddy can I have… and the answer is always YES!

Somehow, even with all of this. Having everything she wants when she wants it, she is still completely boy crazed. She still wants to go to parties and hang out with friends. She even has a boyfriend now.

Desecration of the Black Man
Empress Makeda Gordon

Daddy is about to lose his mind. All he can do to hold on to her is continue to say Yes. By now, that's the only time she gives him time, love, and affection anymore; with the exception of when she is in trouble with mom.

This relationship carries on well into her adult years. She will always be Daddy's Little Girl. His absolute Princess.

While this relationship seems to be so beautiful, what most of us wish was our story, and dream about for our daughters, truth is, this relationship is debilitating to the woman she will soon become.

As Princess moves away to college, she is taking with her a false sense of the Male-Female relationship. The loving family she grew up knowing is getting ready to grow very cold, and that is IF they don't file for a divorce.

I know, I know, I have painted a picture so perfect that you wonder what could have possibly gone wrong. Maybe you didn't catch the "behind the scenes" of this family dynamic.

Three things have taken place here that is cancerous to the core of the entire family.

First, baby girl has grown up learning to be manipulative to get what she wants. She is irresponsible due to her belief that NO MATTER what I do, or what happens to me, my Daddy can fix it, so I can do what I want. She has also NOT learned how to earn anything in life. Her expectations will be that everything she wants should just be given without even having to ask. She will also have an inflated sense of self-worth,

Desecration of the Black Man
Empress Makeda Gordon

because she has been praised her entire life; while her shortcomings were swept under the rug and accepted or excused.

No man this woman ever meets will be good enough. No matter how hard he tries. She will play with his heart and treat him like an ATM. God forbid he ever tells her No, she will not even know what that means coming from a male. And when she ceases to get what she feels she needs from the relationship, she will dispose of him without regard. Because in her heart, she truly believes that she is the best thing since sliced bread. After all, she was treated and attended to better than the woman that gave her life. That has to mean something significant, right?

That brings me to the second point, What about Mom?

Mom has played second fiddle to her very own daughter from the day she brought her home. Not to mention how her authority has been undermined for years by now. She was not granted the opportunity to assist in the molding of her own daughter's life. She has taken a permanent back seat.

The resentment that is brewing under the surface as she puts on her smile for the world, and plays her part, and very well if I might add, is a full falsehood of reality.

She has not only grown to resent her husband but her daughter as well. Because in her mind, it is as if the daughter became the wife and she the concubine. Not in a perverted way, but this is how she feels.

Even if she bore sons prior to having the daughter, once she brought her into this world, all of her husband's love, attentiveness, efforts, and energy went to his Princess. He hardly had anything left to give his wife at the end of any given day. Until his sexual needs reared their little heads up; then, and only then did he shift that passion toward his wife.

Her relationship with her daughter is beyond strained, it is almost non-existent. They don't see eye to eye on anything. The Daughter doesn't trust mother because she was never given a chance to. She was taught through Daddy's actions that Mom was an irrelevant being in the home. She was there to serve only.

The little Princess does not respect her mother at all. She loves her but doesn't respect her. And for that reason alone, she will never learn from a woman what womanhood truly is.

Finally, my third point.

After all of his blood, sweat, and tears that he has poured into his daughter, he forgot one key point, SHE HAS HER OWN LIFE TO LIVE.

Many fathers never take into account that their daughters will grow up, move out, get married, and simply go their own way at some point in their early adulthood.

Letting Go, for this type of father is extremely hard to do. He has committed his life, in a sense, to his Princess; just for her to up and leave him, and make other men priorities over him.

Desecration of the Black Man
Empress Makeda Gordon

Now she is gone, he has become so far removed from his wife and is at a loss as to what value his life has now.

As a protector, men have a need to lead, guide and protect. When there is no one there for him to give that to, he naturally feels less than.

So he finally turns to his wife, who has emotionally left the relationship years ago; ultimately being rejected by her, because she has nothing left to give. He has not acknowledged her existence, in any valuable way, for the last twenty plus years, so their marriage is null and empty.

This scenario will end up in one of three ways:

- A. The couple will agree to live a miserable life together for the sake of being "used to" each other.

- B. The couple will divorce/separate due to irreconcilable differences. They will realize that they have grown too far apart to even want to fix it.
- C. Ideally, they will work it out and be able to move forward successfully.

Regardless of which one they choose, they have released a man-eater out into the world that will be crushing hearts and bleeding bank accounts. She is on the loose and coming for your son. BeWare!

Desecration of the Black Man
Empress Makeda Gordon

So, what is she to do now that she is all grown up?

The majority of us have no clue what that last Daddy image looks like, outside of "The Cosby Show", and other sitcoms like it. So, I want to give you another case study to consider. The Absentee Daddy.

The Absentee Daddy title is not determined by whether or not he is in your life; he is categorized by his interaction with you. Completely gone, an alcoholic, a whoremonger or partier, the hermit or maybe just a workaholic trying to make ends meet at home; the list goes on and on for this type of father. Unfortunately, this is exactly the type that most black women grew up with.

Now, of course, the "deadbeat" (nowhere to be found) is an easy choice, but we all know how that story ends. There was nothing to ever glean from him, therefore, she uses a trial and error method in every relationship forward, with no ability to be reasonable, because she does not know how to relate to men of meaning, AT ALL. It takes a very special man to be able to help this type of woman. But know that there will be many casualties along the road to recovery.

I want to choose the physically present but mentally and emotionally absent father now.

This is the man that always has a reason to NOT invest time with you i.e. he works long hours, he wants to maintain his freedom, he has another woman or family, he's too lazy, and so on and so on. It doesn't even matter, HE IS TOXIC!

Desecration of the Black Man
Empress Makeda Gordon

So, baby girl sees her Daddy on a regular basis or at least has access to him. But he is very consumed with his own life. His needs will trump hers every time.

When she was an infant, she did not understand who wasn't there, only who was. But, as she got older, moving from toddler to school age, she starts to have questions. Mommy has introduced her to her father, she knows who he is. But what she doesn't know is where he is.

Every time Daddy sees her, he makes a big "to do list". He brings gifts and takes her places and she absolutely loves him. When the two of them do get time, it is the most fun she's ever had. Oh, how they laughed and played; she even gets to see all of his side of the family; it is awesome.

But as she grows older, she starts to realize, that she wants more, she needs more from her father.

She begins to evaluate her life; to realize that, yes, Daddy is so much fun, but why did I only get to spend time with him once maybe twice a year. All the rest of the time, he was too busy.

She now starts noticing the look on her mother's face every time he comes around or someone even mentions his name. She starts to remember all of the quiet arguments her parents would have about her, all of the times he made promises that he did not keep, and the things she needed but he never came through for her.

Desecration of the Black Man
Empress Makeda Gordon

Yet, somehow, mom always had a plate of food ready for him when she knew he was coming. This is confusing to a child.

All the nights of them arguing in the bedroom; moving from semi loud voices to a secret parent language that could never be decoded, because it was all sounds and no words, confused her even more. Afterward, Daddy would just leave and Mommy would cry.

By the time she hits her teenage years, she is fully aware and has come up with her own judgments of her Daddy.

Maybe it was his constant lies or the way he made her momma feel. Perhaps it was her seeing the difference between how her sibling's daddies were, versus hers; or even the little games daddy used to play with her that hurt and made her afraid.

Whatever the reasons were, she decided not to trust him, not to depend on him, and to definitely guard her heart concerning him.

There is no Princess in this scenario. Just a "Rejected One".

The "Rejected One" is going to have a boatload of bad friendships and relationships. Simply because there is no clarity on what that male-female relationship looks like. She, unlike the Princess, will get her heart broken more than she will break hearts. Her heart is still very tender. She didn't learn how to "not care" like Princess did; she had a void, a longing to be loved and accepted.

As women, we have an innate need to give. And give is what she does well; to anyone and everyone in the hopes that she can fill the emptiness in her heart. There's only one problem, she doesn't have any idea what a worthy male looks like. So she throws her heart and her body into every single one that crosses her path.

The Rejected One, yearns to Not be rejected. She works very hard to "get it right", to prove to herself that she is lovable. And sometimes she succeeds; but when she does, she doesn't know what to do with it, so she starts to pull back a bit. She starts fights and pushes him away. Why? Because she remembers that men come, but they don't stay, so she guards her heart against the tears her mother cried. But, when she comes across the ones that use and abuse her, she feels right at home and labors long with them. All the way up until they leave her crushed. Which only cosigns her belief in the former, men come but do not stay.

For the little girls that have that Daddy that comes home every night but is disconnected from his family, she learns from him too. She learns that, as long as he is here, I will not rock the boat. I mean, at least he is staying, that is more than she could say for her Daddy.

The moral of both stories is that hurt people, hurt people.

Desecration of the Black Man
Empress Makeda Gordon

The good men that each of these Daughter Types encountered in their lives, walked away injured.

They were injured because they dared to love a woman with no clarity of what love was. While each of the Daddy's loved their Daughters, none of them gave them a foundation for what they can realistically expect and require from a man.

Therefore, she took the good man for granted and damaged his heart.

Whether or not he will ever be able to give on that level again, we will never know. That will be the next woman's battle.

It is so imperative that we take the time to evaluate our "Daddy Relationships" and see if we are walking around holding men to, or making them pay for what our Daddies did or didn't do. We must also realize that "Daddy Relationships" are not limited to biological connection. It could also be your Uncle or Step Father, as well as any other man that has played the "Daddy Roll" in your life. These men, collectively are the pieces to a complete puzzle.

If you have an opportunity to go back and give some of those broken hearts peace, do so. If not, be mindful of our brothers bleeding. Be the example that restores their faith in the Black Woman.

Sibling Rivalry

Chapter Two

She's his first female peer. The one that he will eventually use as a measuring gauge to draw information on every girl within his age group. He may be older and she is his little sister, or vice versa.

If he is the elder sibling, he will be very protective from the day she comes home. This behavior carries over to adolecents and through adulthood. "Big Brothers" take pride in being the big guy. It feeds their natural "Protector Attribute". He tends to take some form of responsibility for her trauma and the effects that it has on her life. The idea of not being able to shield her from harm directly effects his esteem as a male/man. It subconsciously speaks to inadequacy. That inadequacy shows itself later in life as either extreme aggression or fear of confrontation with people in general.

As the younger, he resents her presence here on this earth; he sees her as a replacement child. The baby- Toddler relationship is strained from the moment mommy brings her home. She gets all of the attention and what he considers love.

Desecration of the Black Man
Empress Makeda Gordon

She is an infant and needs much more focus. But, it is virtually impossible for him to understand that.

As time goes on, he begins to not only love her, but he becomes the "Big Brother", her protector. This is a natural and very common transition for men.

He doesn't like anyone to touch her or even come near her; she is his baby. His parent(s) have continuously told him how he has to look out for her. It is his job to make sure she is always ok. And he takes his job very seriously.

They grow up a bit and now baby sis is getting ready to start attending his school. He, hmm, let's call him James and her Lizzy.

James is a bit confused about how he feels about her invading his domain. I mean, she already played with all of his toys and shared a room with him at home. But he sucks it up, knowing there really isn't anything he can do about it, so he accepts it. When in actuality, he doesn't want her in his space because he has seen some unpleasant things that concerns him about her being there.

James and Lizzy are two years apart.

This space gives him comfort because she is not directly in his path at school. But he doesn't forget his "job"; James is still very protective of his little sister and refuses to allow anything to happen to her.

Desecration of the Black Man
Empress Makeda Gordon

One day in middle school, a boy decided that he was going to tease Lizzy in front of everybody in the school yard and James immediately comes to her rescue. He gets right up in the boy's face and pulled his arm back as far as he could and POW, before anyone could stop him, James had punched the boy right in the face.

Of course, he got in a world of trouble at school, and even got suspended.

But at home, he was praised for "doing the right thing" by protecting his sister. Mom could not stop raving about how happy she was that he took care of Lizzy, and Dad, well Dad had the proudest look on his face. He even rewarded James by allowing him to tag along as he went out to meet up with some friends.

His father could not wait to brag to his friends about how his son don't take no mess. Dad and his friends all high fived James, rubbed his head vigorously and even felt that he had earned his first sip of beer. Without mom's knowledge, of course.

James took it all in. He had decided that day, at age twelve, that he was going to continue to be a protector because he absolutely loved all of the attention he was getting. Not to mention, in that moment that he had hit that boy, he experienced a feeling of extreme aggression. It was a rush to him. It felt so good.

As the years pass by, and James and Lizzy move into high school, it gets worst. Now she is so boy crazy and that it is driving him nuts. She has the worst choices in boyfriends, according to him, and she just won't listen. He is growing tired of this Protective Roll that he was roped into, but there is nothing he can do about it. It has become as much a part of his life as waking up and brushing his teeth.

At home, one evening, James overhears a conversation of Lizzy on the phone with a guy. At first, he didn't pay it very much attention because she was being her usual mushy self; I love you, I miss you, I can't wait to see you... blah blah blah. And then it happened, he heard her say the name "Mike". James had the most perplexed look on his face because he was sure her boyfriend's name was Nate.

After that call, James went to Lizzy and asked, "Hey sis, did you and Nate break up"? She looked at him smiling and asked "Why". James tells her "I could have sworn I heard you call him Mike". She replies, "I did. I wasn't talking to Nate, I was talking to Mike, you know Mike from the church, Sister Smith's son. He is so cute and I really like him".

James just looked at her with disgust. Then asked, "well does Nate know that you are talking to Mike? Are you going to tell him?" She looked at him with the most intense look on her face as she walked up to him and grabbed his arms and said "No he doesn't know, I'm not sure what I want to do yet. Please don't tell him, I need to figure things out first and then I will decide who I want to be with, then I'll let the other one go." James says ok and heads to his room.

Desecration of the Black Man
Empress Makeda Gordon

Later that night, He couldn't stop his sister's situation from creeping into his thoughts. He began a dialogue in his head.

He said to himself;

Nate is a real cool dude. He plays on my football team. It seemed like they were getting along well. Well I know he really loves her. He told me so himself, and he knows I don't play about Lizzy.

Then he thought…

How could Lizzy be talking to two guys at the same time and telling them both the same exact thing? What is she trying to figure out if she is already telling this Mike guy that she Loves him?

Question after Question entered his head. So many that he had a very hard time getting to sleep that night. All he knew was his sister was a good girl and that is why he has created this fortress around her. Everyone knew not to mess with her. So he did not understand how Mike slipped under his radar.

After about a week, James just let it go and moved on. He had concluded that Lizzy was stubborn and was going to do what she wanted to do. He knew his sister well. And at the end of the day, he wanted her to be happy, so if that meant dating them both to be sure, then so be it.

James watched Lizzy continue this same behavior with different guys all throughout high school. He had just decided that his sister was a player and rationalized it by saying, "that's just Lizzy". So, he went on with his own dating life.

When James was about twenty-two years old, He met a young woman that he really liked. She was beautiful, intelligent and had the "body of life", as he called it. Her name was Candice.

Candice had James feeling things for a woman that he had never felt. She introduced him to so many new things, such as; African culture, and thinking about his future and what it would entail. She had James making life goals. Something he has never done before.

She stimulated him. He was interested in so much more then her body by now. James was actually beginning to fall in love.

After a couple of months of dating, James brought Candice home to meet his family. Everyone loved her. Mom was being her normal embarrassing self, talking about how pretty her grandchildren would be; Dad was so proud that she was such a "hottie", and then there was Lizzy. Let's just say that Lizzy was Not thrilled about her big brother getting all caught up with "some girl".

She did not hesitate to give Candice the cold shoulder. Her maternal instincts kicked in full force, you could tell by how she was grilling poor Candice so harshly. Ignoring all of James' pleading with her.

Eventually, she laid off and decided to leave the house.

It's been almost a year now and James and Candice are going strong. Candice's older brother is coming home from the Military and her family is having dinner party for him. This will be James' first time meeting Rob.

Dinner is going well. Everyone is having a great time. Afterward, the whole family moves to the living room to continue enjoying each other's company.

Rob, Candice's brother, starts telling stories to James about when they were kids. He went on and on about how she was such a confused young girl. She could never make a decision. Then he said it, Rob said; Her excuse was always that she was trying to "figure things out".

That one statement sent James' mind on a trip down memory lane. He was no longer listening to what was being said, he was now full throttle in his own thoughts about his little sister Lizzy. He remembered how that was always her excuse, hell it still is.

He thought…

Lizzy was sweet, just like Candice; she was intelligent, just like Candice; She was beautiful, just…like…Candice. He took the deepest breath ever.

Desecration of the Black Man
Empress Makeda Gordon

"James, James, JAMES!" Candice called out. Oh! "I'm sorry baby", he replied. "I must have spaced out".

James made up an excuse to leave. He needed to get out of there right then. So he did. And he rushed home to talk to Lizzy.

He ran to his sister's room, stopped at the closed door, took a deep breath to calm himself, then he knocked. "Come in", Lizzy responded. James walked in and sat on the bed and asked if he could ask her some questions. "Of course", she replied. After all, they had a very close relationship.

Surprisingly, none of his questions were about Lizzy directly. He poured out every question he had about women in general. You would think that mom would have been a better person to talk to because of her life's experience being older and more mature, but she always made things "awkward" so he didn't want to talk to her. James felt that he and Lizzy were in the same generation so she would have more to offer a man his age.

Never once did he give thought to the fact that Lizzy was only a twenty-one-year-old woman who was enjoying life and has never been faithful or committed to a guy in her life. All he saw was the commonalities between her and Candice that were revealed at dinner earlier that evening.

They talked for hours about a little of everything. She told him about how she falls for a guy, what she does when she is over one, what makes her "overlap" relationships, so on and so

Desecration of the Black Man
Empress Makeda Gordon

on. Every emotion entered that room through that one conversation.

At about 2 AM, James finally went to his room to go to bed. He laid down feeling that he now had all the answers to how women are and how they think. Thanks to baby sis, so he thought.

The very next day, James woke up and his entire relationship with Candice was changed. He met up with Candice for dinner and a movie. During dinner, he looked up at her and something was different about her. He couldn't put his finger on it, but he knew she did not look the same to him.

Staring at her creepily, Candice asked, what's wrong baby? He continued to stare. Then replied, Nothing, I'm good.

Just behind Candice, a waitress was walking up and caught James' eye. She smiled at him and winked. James tried to look away and ignore her. Unfortunately, she was their waitress.

She approached the table and looked right at him with the biggest smile, never once acknowledging Candice's presence, and says, "Hi, I'm Simone, can I start you off with something to drink?". Candice felt her disrespect and answered, ordering for the both of them; as James pretended to be texting someone in order to stay out of trouble.

By the end of dinner, the waitress had noticed that her advances were not received well, so she did what any woman would do (according to his sister), She wrote her number on the back of the bill and gave it to him. Candice did not notice a thing.

Later on that night, while James laid in bed, he stared at that receipt with the phone number. Not because he was contemplating calling her, he really loved Candice, but because he now has sound evidence that Lizzy was right about how sneaky women can be when they want to. This disturbed him greatly.

Needless to say, in less than two months, Candice and James were no more. His trust went completely out the window and she had had enough.

Over the next few years, Lizzy had one bad break up after the next. The tables had turned for her and she began to be the one getting cheated on repeatedly. Between her own indiscretions that she had gotten away with and the ones she had been enduring, she quickly developed an enormous distrust for women in general. Yet, James continued to consult with her and have her screen all of his love interest. No one could tell him that his sister did not have his back. She had hipped him to game, in his mind, and continues to do so.

The problem with this is, Lizzy was dysfunctional in the love zone, and very bias when judging women. She never intended to mislead him. She honestly thought that she was "looking out" for her brother. She believed her own lies.

James went well into his twenties taking her advice and failing at every relationship he tried. He never understood why. So he eventually put up a stone wall that no woman could enter. From that day forward, James used women for his pleasure, the same way he was taught to believe they had been doing with him.

The challenge with this is that he was receiving bad counsel. The relationship he had with his sister was one built on love and trust. Neither of the two realized that they both were operating from a damaged perspective on love. Lizzy never realized that her actions spoken and unspoken were creating a measuring bar for her brother. It was never her intent to hurt him. In her mind, she was "keeping it 100" with him.

With all of the parental lessons that they received about taking care of eachother, neither James nor Lizzy was taught accountability for one another. They did what most do, which is give what they have without gaining more along the way.

"HURT PEOPLE, HURT PEOPLE. EVEN WHEN THEY DON'T MEAN TO".

Mother, May I

Chapter Three

8 pounds, 6 ounces, and 23 inches long, my beloved, my Son. This is the happiest day of a parent's life. In a Mother's Life.

As a father, this is such a proud moment. He vows to make him strong and well rounded. He vows to make a "man" of him. As a mother, her instinctive nurturer rears its head. She instantly wants to give him as much love as she has and protect him from the evils of this world. This is her opportunity to release into society the "truth" of what a man should be. Both parents have the best and purest intent towards their gift.

She takes him home and holds him, stares at him continuously. She feels a love inside of herself like she has never felt. She talks to him and plays with him. Whispers all sorts of promises to him as he sleeps. She calls his name, Stephen, and swears that she will never let anything happen to him.

Desecration of the Black Man
Empress Makeda Gordon

As Stephen grows into the toddler stage, he is very inquisitive and explorative. His energy is endless. Stop, No, Don't... her vocabulary has been dominated by these words. Yet, somehow, he still can do no wrong in her eyes. He breaks the lamp, fights his sister, jumps off of things, and even fights mom; "but he is just a baby, he doesn't know better", mom cries.

His beginning of learning "right from wrong" has begun. His little brain retains that some things he does are a "no, no", but there is no reprocusion to doing them anyway.

The Urban community generally calls for mothers to return to work at some point after the baby is born. Putting the child in a daycare of sorts is the only option. Her guard goes up almost immediately and the protective instincts move to the forefront of her mind. She knows her child very well and will defend him at all cost.

At age 3-4 years old, our children become a bit more independent. Their minds are beginning to make decisions that are thought out verses just instinctual. They know, feel, and understand on a higher level now. Each thing that is learned and executed in the outside world (outside the home) is only what is executed within the home; with the complexity being their lack of knowledge of "outside" rules.

One day one of Stephen's teachers observe him hitting another child because this child will not give him the toy that she is playing with. Stephen hits her and takes the toy away. The teacher goes over to Stephen and tells him that "that isn't

Desecration of the Black Man
Empress Makeda Gordon

nice", and he should not hit. He should ask nicely. Stephen says okay, so the teacher returns to doing what she needs to do for the other children. Suddenly, she hears a sharp scream, and one of the other teachers rushed over to Stephen. Stephen had pushed the same little girl down to the floor and she was injured. The teacher who originally addressed Stephen then puts him in the "time out" chair. He is hysterically crying.

Less than 5 minutes later, mom walks in and sees her son so upset. The teacher attempts to explain to mom why Stephen is in time out, but she is abruptly interrupted as mom is rushing to him. She picks Stephen up and storms up to the teacher yelling at her. The teacher explains, wherever she can get a word in, then asks mom to sign an incident report, which has to be given to the little girl's parents, about her injury. As the mother refused to sign the form, she continues to tell the teachers what they will and will not do with her son. She insists that he is a little boy and little boys are rough, and how they should know that.

What this mother is not realizing is that she has not prepared her son with basic peer interaction skills. His aggression toward his siblings at home is accepted and sometimes even co-signed through laughter. She has an expectation that in the free world her son should be treated as he is in the comfort of his home.

The biggest lesson that Stephen can walk away with from this situation, what he will remember most, is how his mother punished those who punished him, and she continues to do so without pause. She even comes to his aid concerning the attempts of discipline that his father makes.

Over the years, she continuously makes excuses for his sketchy behaviors in school and conspires with her son to hide things from his father. All to ultimately "keep him safe" from discipline. She sees no wrong in him. On the few occasions that she does, and tries to address it with Stephen, he plays on her emotions and gets out of it every time.

As Stephen moves into his teenaged years, he is becoming a handful to say the least. He is exhibiting all of the normal teen rebellion behaviors, but he has a twist to his. He does not believe in the basic concept of "Cause and Effect". But how could he? He has never had to feel any effects from anything he has caused.

He is growing up so fast that mom can't handle him. He is now interacting with friends more than her. She misses him, so she finds ways to feel close to him. At sixteen years old, Stephen has never even cleaned his own room. She cooks and cleans and does all of his laundry. He has absolutely no domestic skills AT ALL. But doing those things for him makes her feel as if she is still needed. In addition, she gives him everything he asks for. No matter if she can afford it or not, she finds a way. And she takes his smiles, thank yous, and kisses as currency.

Clearly, mom is his rock, or "favorite person" in the world. Anything that is hard in his life, be it trouble that he

Desecration of the Black Man
Empress Makeda Gordon

Gets himself into or decisions he needs to make, "Super Mom" swoops in and handles it all.

This is the life of Stephen!

Once Stephen becomes an adult and is now feeling ready to take on his own family, he walks out of his mother's house. He is turned over to a woman who has no idea what she is truly getting as a husband.

He is well versed in the art of "Wooing" a woman. He has done it with his mother his entire life. He captures the woman's heart through his application of affections and attentiveness. He makes her feel secure and needed, constantly, because he actually does need her.

What she does not know about her man is that he is missing some key components to an adult relationship. What he does not know is how many failed relationships he will endure due to his inflated view of his self-worth. Not to say that he is not a good guy, but, your worth is based on your value. And when you have nothing to bring to the table, you bring no value to your relationship.

There is such thing as Cause and Effect of "Over Mothering", "Over Compensating", "Over Nurturing", "Over Validating", and so on and so on, to a son. As mothers, we are given a responsibility to aid in the preparation of our children to be productive individuals, co-existing, in this realm.

Desecration of the Black Man
Empress Makeda Gordon

As Mothers, we have to realize that we are raising someones Husband, Father, Employee, etc. If we do not keep this Truth in mind, we will fall into the catergory of raising a Man for ourselves. We make him what WE need versus what the world needs.

If we were to look at Stephen's upbringing and correlate it to his adult life, it would look something like this…

Cause	*Effect*
No distinction of "Good & Bad" Behavior	Self-Absorption, Self-Gratification
Cleaning up all the messes	Irresponsibility, Inability to think independently
Covering/Hiding Errors	Manipulative Behaviors, Dishonesty
Codling	Dependency, Need for Validation
No domestic Responsibility	No Work Ethic, Objectification of people

Desecration of the Black Man
Empress Makeda Gordon

The questions I would venture to ask here is, would you choose the man on the right as your husband? And if you learn later, that the man you chose, was in fact, the man on the right, how happy would you be in that union? If you would not be happy, think about who and what you are presenting to the world and to a potential wife when raising a son this way. However, if you are okay with this type of man, you have to evaluate your "co-depency meter".

And I have not even touched on the flip side of this coin, which is the "Mama's Boy". The little boy parading around in a grown man's body but has not been weened. The son that cannot or will not make a single life decision without his mother's opinion and/or approval, and mom loves it that way. His entire life is molded and being maintained by his mother.

Even when he chooses a wife, she has been approved by his mother and is turned over to his mother after matrimony to be molded into mom for his further pacification.

Then, for the men who venture out and choose their own, against his mother's judgment, well that woman is in for a life of misery. Mom will make sure that she never feels accepted, that she "knows" that she is and will never be good enough for her son. While he sits on the sidelines and stays quiet. After all, at his core, he is incapable of truly going against his "mommy".

As women of mature age (thirty years and older), it is likely that we have experienced, not one, but both of these "Mother, May I" type of men. Yet we continuously recreate them. Why is that?

Desecration of the Black Man
Empress Makeda Gordon

We do our sons a disservice by not effectively carrying out the blessed task we were given.

As a Black Man in this world, he is born with a societal disadvantage. Why are we so oblivious to our contribution of making their plight more difficult? Why are we not imparting strength through the morals and values we know to be right?

We send them out into this world, that is so cruel to them, without any defense. We compile their woes in Life and Love by what we DO and DO NOT teach. They are ever learning, so "What" are you teaching?

A woman who does not see a man's worth does not have the tools needed to give her son what is needed to be a man from the feminine perspective. She will raise him to be what "she wants" in a man or she will neglect to raise him because she has no respect for men in general. In both cases, the future of that particular young man is doomed, unless a man steps in and corrects her wrong.

The double standard that we as women are delusional about, yet we live by is: "A man is only as strong as the Queen that stands behind him", but then we are raising sons that don't know how to lean on, or cleave to His Queen because you have consciously or subconsciously appointed yourself the Only Queen that matters. How does the Black Community move forward with a lasting change, if we are not equipping the next generation to carry the torch?

The "EASY" Life

Chapter Four

Ladies Night Out, he spots her from across the room. He sends her and her friends a drink and just like that, it begins. Kendall and Sean have "chemistry".

As the evening progresses, they stay by each other's side. You would have thought that they had been together forever. The way he looked at her, the smiles she gave to him; it felt so good to them both. The evening ends in passionate lovemaking followed by a rush to depart.

As the weeks go by, the two are inseparable. They disclosed on the first real date that each of them had a "situation", or what the rest of us call being in a Relationship. Both expressing their unhappiness with their perspective partners. Sharing stories of misery and obligations. The dysfunction became their bond.

There was no pressure for either of them to leave their homes. They just enjoyed what they had together. No rules, no accountability, no obligations, simply... "The EASY Life".

Desecration of the Black Man
Empress Makeda Gordon

Kendall would often confide in Sean when she and her boyfriend would fight. He's mean, He's a liar, He's abusive, and the list goes on. When in fact she had a loving and devoted boyfriend; but she needed a justification to make her feel better about her infidelity. Sean would listen to all of her problems intently and then make love to her to take all of her pain away for the moment. He had grown very fond of her, but still had no intentions of starting a life with her.

This affair is still going strong six months later. They continued to spend every free moment that they could find together.

For Sean it was easy, he would simply tell his girlfriend that he was going out and would be back. She had stopped questioning him years ago. She knew the man she was with. She knew he was a cheater; she had caught him many times over the years. So she was numb to it, that stance allowed him to continue to live the lifestyle he chose for himself and for her.

On the other hand, it was not as simple for Kendall. They would laugh at all of her elaborate stories that she had to come up with to get away and be with him. He admired her broadness of imagination. After all, he was the beneficiary of each and every one of those lies.

It's been nearing a year now that this steamy romance has been going on, they had even begun to exchange "I Love You". Things began to get a bit complicated. Kendall now wants more. As disturbing as this was to Sean, he managed to keep her at bay.

Desecration of the Black Man
Empress Makeda Gordon

The more she pushed, the more he pulled back. She had even gone as far as to leave her boyfriend and make herself completely available to him. Annoyed by her decision, Sean decided it was time to let things cool off. He decided that they needed a break from each other. Kendall was devastated. Her boyfriend would not take her back and her lover had rejected her. But still, she held on and decided that she would give Sean time.

Two weeks after the breakup, Kendall's friends decide that she needs to get out of the house. So they head out.

Upon arrival to a party, she goes straight to the bar for a drink and who does she run into? That's right, it's Sean! He is in the same spot, doing the same thing he did when they met. The only difference was that there was now another woman on his arm.

He looked at her the same way, touched her the same way, so she had to assume that he was saying all of the same things to her. She was heartbroken.

Sean spots her and waves with a smile on his face as if she was one of his "homegirls". The overwhelming feeling she was having, drove her right out of the party.

Sean continued to live his life according to his pleasure. Giving regard to no one's feelings but his own.

It wasn't until he felt he needed a break from the energy needed to balance his many women, that he decided to stay home for a while. He slipped right back into the "family life" as if he had never deviated. Life was serene for a few weeks. But then…

Sean's longterm girlfriend took advantage of having him home more often. She started to go out a bit herself. He had no problem with it, initially. He just stayed home with his children.

She started out with lunches and dinners with her girlfriends and then escalated to night clubs occasionally. Sean was just enjoying his peace of mind. Not having to argue and fight about his infidelities for a while was bliss.

A couple of months go by and "Wifey" is preparing for one of her nights out. Sean asked her if they could just chill in the house that evening. Her response floored him. She gave him one of the very same excuses that Kendall once told him she had given her boyfriend. He immediately became enraged. She ignored his aggression and headed out the door.

He had no peace that night. All he could think of was, who his woman was laying underneath.

He watched the clock like a hawk. There was nothing he could do because the children were in bed asleep. He was left alone with his thoughts all night.

He then began to reminisce about past conversations that he and Wifey had. He identified everything she had ever said that was in line with what he had known about Kendall. He realized that he had never stayed with a "side chick" as long as

Desecration of the Black Man
Empress Makeda Gordon

he did Kendall, so he wasn't around long enough to hear the excuses women give.

As he sat there, connecting the dots, he had convinced himself that his woman was definitely cheating on him. When in fact, she wasn't. She had been telling him the truth. But he could not see past what he feels he "knows" about women. Based on his own choices and what he learned through his mistresses.

Life in Sean's house became complete mayhem over the next year. Ultimately, the relationship became irreconcilable, so they parted ways. She, the woman that has stood by his side, put up with all of his indiscretions, reared his children and remained not only faithful but loyal also for more than 5 years, took the children and left him to his vices.

How does this situation affect men and how they love and view women? While we know that both Sean and Kendall were responsible, individually, for their actions, what could have been done differently to build a brother rather than play a part in damaging him?

In this society that we live in today, it is unfortunate, but a reality, that that type of relationship (side pieces) has become "the norm".

Desecration of the Black Man
Empress Makeda Gordon

I'd like to point out a few things that we as women, can do or change about ourselves that will command a higher standard from our brothers, lovers, spouses, and every other black man that crosses our path.

First, you have to understand that you, as a woman hold the power of the Yoni (vagina). No man would ever be able to commit such acts of betrayal, without someone to do it with. We get to make the decision who we lay with. We also have the power to empower our Sister and cover her, even when her man doesn't.

So, what did Sean ultimately learn from Kendall, even though he has been a cheater most of his life? He learned how "Easy" it is for a woman to do what men do, and in some cases, better. Kendall got away with her infidelity for quite some time. And her sharing her tactics with him planted seeds of deceit concerning women. Although he was cheating also, he was now exposed to how the coin has two sides.

Now I am sure that most will feel like "that's on him". But, what we are not taking into account is the "wife/girlfriend" and most important of all, those children. The children are the one's who are affected the most in these situations. As adults, the majority of us have some sort of coping mechanism that allows us to accept and move past the lost of a relationship. But that isn't true for children. All they know is that their father or mother is no longer home.

Desecration of the Black Man
Empress Makeda Gordon

We do realize two very important things; Kendall did not make him the man he is, he was a philanderer when she met him; and secondly, Kendall could have used her power for good. But she was self-serving from whatever her life had encountered; and again, hurt people, hurt people.

In general, Kendall ended up being a hard lesson for Sean. She destroyed his trust in women. Although he was very unfaithly and totally wrong, he never thought that women were capable of such actions before her. He had never seen the error of his ways until Kendall stepped on the scene, and it all backfired on him. She was indeed his lesson. A lesson that he truly needed to learn.

He was unable to learn from his own mistakes. But what he got from his relationship with Kendall was his new-found perception of women in general. While we are crystal clear that he was not the best catch, the portrait that Kendall painted of us as women, has given him or co-signed his perception of who the Black Woman is.

Now I know, I know, that taking any responsibility for the tearing apart of a family and robbing a child or children of the opportunity to grow up in a two parent home is extremely hard to own, we have to. In order to grow, we must identify and nullify our sketchy behaviors that are damaging to our community. Just because a negative thing exist doesn't mean that we have to be a party to it.

Desecration of the Black Man
Empress Makeda Gordon

Can this challenge with black men being unfaithful ever end? The answer is Yes! However, the better question is, is it likely that it will? Probably not, because, we, as Sisters, as Black women are not unified. We do not have a collective code that we all live by, that enforces monogamy. We speak of a code and possibly live by one. The challenge in the code is that it does not seem to apply to women we do not know.

Our communities are disassembled because of our distrust, and disloyalty to one another. Men to men and women to women, and us all toward Our Children.

Imagine a community of women who Honored one another to the point that we Do Not, Will Not, harm each other for any reason, under any circumstance.

What if we looked at a brother that approaches us and has a woman, and simply said NO! No because we honored the sister that was at home, even if he didn't. We not only respected Her, but we thought of the damage we could cause to her children by facilitating the existence of their broken home.

Even with Sean having the "dog" in him that he had, if there was no one willing to engage with him, what would he accomplish? Nothing at all.

We need to send Fathers Home.

Kendall's first mistake was looking outside of her relationship to fix whatever was going on inside of it. She took a good man (her man) and damaged him. He is damaged because she became more Self-Involved than Unit-Involved.

Desecration of the Black Man
Empress Makeda Gordon

She played a part in killing one man's faith in Loyalty while simultaneously co-signing another man's belief that women are not worthy of trust. That part was all her.

Now, these things may not have ever crossed her mind in any intentional way, but her lack of discipline and guidance accomplished the task anyway. This is why we all need a Mentor. Not just a friend to listen, but someone detached from our lives with wisdom and the ability to develop us in our areas of weakness. Some of us don't do better because we don't know better. That is why we need to be teachable.

In relationships, Married, or Single, there is a decorum that we as women must share if we want to get the best out of our Brothers. We must create the image that we want to be seen in. The communal climate we want to live in.

It is a fact that Kendall destroyed her boyfriend's faith in women because he gave parts of himself that he had never given to another woman in a relationship. She took his vulnerability and trampled all over it. Chances are, he may never feel safe in a relationship again. These types of behaviors, when we do not respect our men's trust in us, begins to set a mental stigma that affects black women as a whole. And conducting yourself in a manner that is not "Communally Conscious" is perpetualting the stigma that we black women already have to combat in our day to day lives.

For some men, it only takes one heartbreak to damage them for many years, if not forever, and for others, it may take a few heartbreaks. But what we do Know is that each one is affecting him deeply both mentally and emotionally. And these men become father's that raise sons that marry daughters. There inlies "The Vicious Cycle".

Our breakdown in the "Sisterhood" between Black Women everywhere, is an intricate part of what is happening to our Black Men.

Everything between us has become competitive. We are so focused on the petty things such as who dresses the best, who drives the best car, who has the best house, etc., that we are not being attentive to what really matters, Our Families, The Family Unit. We are so busy coveting our Sister's life that we lack the ability to celebrate her as we create our own.

The moment We become "My Sister's Keeper" again, is the moment we begin to heal Our Nation within the Nation. We are maternal, with or without children; so, we need to operate as mothers; concerning the children within our communities. Therefore, as we are growing to regain the place of love and respect for our Sister, let us allow the children to be our "reason" not to create or participate in desecrating the Black Family.

The "Doll House" Syndrome

Chapter Five

The Concubine! Who is She? What is her purpose?

By definition, a concubine is a woman who lives "with" a man, but has a lower status than his wife, she is a mistress of sorts. Sometimes known, but most times unknown.

In today's terms, we call her the "Side Chick". She is not in a relationship with any man but the one that is "keeping" her financially, sexually, mentally, and so on. She is the woman that knows that the man has a woman and/or a family, but wants to be with him, or has a need for him so badly that she is willing to be secondary and kept a secret. She is satisfied by what he provides for her. Be it money, sex, comfort, or maybe just for the sake of not being alone.

Let's explore the life of Lisa and Kevin.

Kevin has been married for nine years and has three children with his wife. Lisa met Kevin six months ago. He was honest and shared his marital status with her; At first she was uncomfortable with it, but soon became tolerant and decided to overlook it.

Desecration of the Black Man
Empress Makeda Gordon

They met in a local grocery store. The moment he laid eyes on her he knew he had to have her. So he approached her. He didn't lead of with "I'm married", of course. He just addressed her with confidence and charm. She found him very attractive as well, so she was open to his approach.

After about a week or so of talking on the phone, they met up for the first time. Kevin took her to a beautiful restaurant, opened all of her doors, brought her flowers and pulled out her chair. Lisa was not used to this behavior, since she has been dating all the "around the way" type of guys. She was very impressed by his manners, care and attentiveness toward her.

Throughout dinner, she couldn't stop staring at him. He was in awe of her also. But he knew that he needed to tell her what she was getting into, so he did. Once he told her that he was married, she was so disappointed. She sat for a minute and gathered herself. Thinking that she had never met a guy so well put together, she told herself, rather convinced herself, that he was there with her because he wasn't happy at home.

That is where it all began.

Lisa started to ask questions about his relationship and why he had approached her. He responded with the slick talk that many men use. You know, I'm not happy, she doesn't understand me, I have one foot out of the door. The usual. Yet, she fell for it. Those words gave her hope that maybe one day she would win his heart and he would be with her. But deep down, she knew it would not be a requirement.

Desecration of the Black Man
Empress Makeda Gordon

As time progresses, the two become an item. Not a couple but an Item. She has nuzzled herself right into his life. And he gladly received her.

Now, to some, this may seem like a pretty good situation. After all, for him, he gets to maintain his current life while adding his "spice" on the side, and she gets to change her relationship status and financial status; in her head anyway.

The challenge is that there is no level of responsibility in this situation. Kevin has his family, which comes first always, while Lisa is reduced to accepting the sloppy seconds. And some part of her tells herself that this is enough, which is the low self-image part, if I may add.

The fact that he has disclosed his relationship status to her relinquishes him from every accountability and validates every excuse he uses to explain his absence and non-focal ability. She has now placed herself in a position to have to take whatever he gives without complaint.

Where things get a little murky is when someone begins to catch feelings, which they will.

After a few months of bliss, Kevin's wife begins to get a bit antsy about his consistent disappearances and things get tight at home. So, what does Kevin do? He refocuses his attention to his wife in an effort to calm her. He is home more and doing more with his family. Meanwhile, he has not let go of Lisa. He just keeps telling her to hold on, that he is working things out so that they can "be together". Lisa takes that term very literally. She is assured that he is closing out that relationship so that he can be with her full time. When in actuality he means, getting back to spending time with her.

What Lisa fails to understand about this so-called relationship is that she is the absolute definition of "Friends with Benefits". She is not his woman, nor his wife; therefore, she is a friend who gives and receives benefits. He satisfies her emotional and physical needs (when he can) and she satisfies his need for an escape. Escape from his reality for a while, the pressures of his real life and responsibilities. He can find peace with Lisa because she is unable to hold him accountable for anything. He will always wiggle his way out of that discussion with one simple phrase, "You knew my situation when we started this". That one statement exonerates him from any and all explaining that would need to be done in an actual relationship. And he would be right. Lisa, in fact, did sign up to be the "afterthought", the "fill in the blanks" woman in his life.

If we were to use the correct terms for what Lisa truly is, it would be a Concubine. She is Lower than, and for his pleasure.

As a wife, there is a voice that is allowed. The man you married took a Vow with you and to you. He made you certain promises in this life that you are building toward together, so she has a right to hold him to his word. As a Concubine, you have no such authority with the man you lay with. He has promised you nothing but some provisions and sex. And most times, those promises are met, until their expiration date. Yes, Expiration Date. A Concubine can be sent away at any time for any reason. He can simply no longer see a need for you, and/or

Desecration of the Black Man
Empress Makeda Gordon

replace you and move on, with or without notice, and you must go. His household will always take precedence over you. His needs will always take precedence over you. Most women in the position of the "Side Chick" forget the "Rules of Engagement".

What this Side Chick does not see is the damage that she is doing to the children that man has at home. She does not acknowledge her participation in the ruins of a family. She can only see her needs.

She has no concern for all the nights that the wife lays in bed and cries herself to sleep; she only sees her tears. She cannot wrap her mind around the fact that the time he is putting in with her could be redirected to being a better father; she only sees that her children need a father figure. She cannot see the food that is being taken out of his children's mouths, the college funds they won't have, nor the sacrifices his wife is making to make ends meet, not knowing that he is spending the family money elsewhere; she only sees that her bills need to be paid. Honestly, neither of them are seeing reality. They are both self-serving, but a man can only do or be what you allow.

Lisa has foregone or is oblivious to the damage that she is causing her community. Her scope of view is narrow. This is where we come up with the illusion that there is a shortage of good men, so we might as well share. When in actuality, if we held our Black Men more accountable they would be home and we would not be left to "do what we gotta do".

Desecration of the Black Man
Empress Makeda Gordon

So do not contribute to the Desecration of the Black Man by being his "Out" from living up to the Royal King that he is.

Now let's talk about "Wifey".

When my husband and I got serious, he called me his wifey. I took offense to that term. I asked him to never call me that again. I was either his woman or his wife; I don't do Wifey. Not because I didn't think it was cute, but because I understood it's meaning. A **WIFEY** means "Serious Girlfriend", "Wife Material", according to the definition. So for me, you cannot, will not refer to me, Your Wife, as a girlfriend or material. I am already chosen!

Many women praise this roll. They think it is an accomplishment in their love life to make it to the "Wifey" level. But a Elevated Woman understands that that term simply means that you are "considering me" not that you have chosen me. There is a huge difference between the two. We seem to take that term as a badge of honor. I disagree. The badge of honor is the ring followed by the vows. Until then, I personally, am not impressed.

Wifey, generally lives with you and has children by you. She has become "A" priority in his life, not "The" priority in his life. The only difference between a "Wifey" and a "Concubine" is that you live in the "Big House". He has decided that you will live under the same roof with him. He trusts you more, so you get the "reward" of bearing his children and sleeping beside him every night. Concubines rarely get that. Well they occasionally get the child, but never the treatment.

You have been given the pleasure of cooking, cleaning, baring his children, paying bills with him, you also get a limited amount of questions per month that you can ask, as well as being seen in public with him. It's like being a Wife with training wheels.

As Wifey, as opposed to a Wife, you get to "Play" wife, but without all benefits. It's kind of like getting a promotion on your job with no increase in pay, but you are trusted with more responsibility, a little more respect, and a better title. And we call this "winning"?

Granted we all have our perception of marriage and how we go about it. For some, it is a big ceremony and for others, it is a vow and commitment. For my faith, it is a vow, commitment, and conviction. Whatever your faith is, Do That. But, make sure that your legalities are in order at the same time. Meaning get the Will and Power of Attorney in place.

Here We Go…

Sonia and Patrick have been together for seven years, living together for five and they also have one child together. Sonia has one child from a former relationship and Patrick has three other children with two separate mothers. Sonia has played a part in his children's lives throughout the entire relationship. Patrick was married to one of his children's mothers and is now divorced. All the women get along fairly well.

Patrick tells Sonia that he isn't ready for another "Marriage" because he is afraid it will fail and they have been doing so good for so many years. Sonia accepts because she has her man.

She does everything that is required, and then some, for her family. She takes good care of Patrick, and his children, as well as their child together. She does all the wifely duties while managing her nine to five job. Life is good.

Patrick gets hurt on the job and can no longer work. Sonia steps up and handles everything. She is a good woman. But marriage is no longer a topic in their home. They are happy, and that is all that matters, Right?

Deep down Sonia wants the wedding that she has always dreamed of but she accepts her life for what it is. Patrick grows frustrated with the state of his life being disabled. He remembers life as it was and is not embracing fully what it has become. But they manage.

A couple of years down the line, Patrick falls sick, and a few months later he passes away. Sonia and his family handle all of the arrangements. They send him off in the most beautiful manner possible. But….

Desecration of the Black Man
Empress Makeda Gordon

Patrick and Sonia never handled the legalities of their relationship. She chose not to hold him to any standard concerning her or her child. She chose to stay Wifey with limited benefits.

When the time came to pay for all of the arrangements, she looked to his life insurance and pension plan to help, but was unsuccessful. Patrick's first wife was still the beneficiary on everything. And she was done pretending.

She tolerated Sonia to keep her at bay. She did not want her to get wind of the secret relationship that she continued to have with Patrick. She knew that he had not changed anything and she kept her mouth closed to keep from any changes being made.

Once the policies were paid out to her and she signed off on the receipt of his pension, there was nothing that Sonia could do. Even though their marriage lasted merely three years and Sonia had been there for ten years at that point, the ex-wife gave nothing to either of his other children's mothers. She took care of her own children with him, and herself.

Sonia was now flat broke, living paycheck to paycheck and had to move into a smaller home to make ends meet. So here we have the Ex-wife living in peace while the one who should have been cared for, and would have seen about them all, struggling. Simply because she refused to hold her man to a standard. She refused to deem herself worthy of having all of the benefits of being his wife. She accepted being Wifey.

Desecration of the Black Man
Empress Makeda Gordon

Now this may sound like Sonia did nothing wrong, or nothing to contribute to the "Desecration" of that brother, but that would be a wrong assessment. She co-signed his fears instead of helping to heal them. She relinquished him of all responsibility to his household to keep the peace. She allowed him to let another woman reap where she had not sown.

In this case, the man passed away. But, how many "Patricks" are still alive and just have moved on after we have committed our lives and gave all we could to them?

Not commanding that a man does as men should do, which is to provide and protect us, condones their failure or complacency. You don't have to be controlling to stand strong. It is often said that the man is the head and the woman the backbone. The backbone, or spine, travels into the neck which guides the heads movement. How are you supporting the head, if you are not stabilizing it?

The moral of this story is that a man will never be, or even see the need to be, any more to you, or himself, than he is right now, until YOU require it. Once we accept his flaws as a part of who he is without attempting to help him heal, we accept Everything that comes with that blockages that he has. He cannot grow into the greatness that he needs to, because we, "Wifey", do not command it. We play the role of a wife without the actuality of being Her.

The only thing a man can learn from this is that he does not have to do better or be better because he is not required to.

Desecration of the Black Man
Empress Makeda Gordon

So he stands in his pain, in his weakness, strongly, with no elevation in sight.

The truth of the value of a woman is in her ability to not lead but guide her family in a manner that solidifies and elevates the family as a unit.

Settling for a "Wifey" position is a disservice to first You, then that Man, which affects the children, leaking into the community. We have to hold our men to the standard that we hold ourselves to. Do not allow yourself to be downplayed or devalued for the sake of not being alone or financial gain. Your integrity and principles are what determines what you attract.

If you find yourself in a Wifey position, step back an re-evaluate you current relationship. If you are giving on a level that you are not receiving, it may be time to let it go. But before you do, sit down and create your own clear and consice standards, then talk it over with your partner. Real Love Is Responsive!

Desecration of the Black Man
Empress Makeda Gordon

Who is Jezebel

Chapter Six

She is Temerarious as a Queen. In her life, she has only learned the most incontinent of wants, thoughts, and behaviors. So indurate is she in the lack of recognizing his kingship that his position is lowered. He no longer makes the calculated steps of a King. Now he only moves in a direction, commanded by her; he is regulated to a bishop. Her power is oppressive, and he is now obsequious to her authority. It doesn't matter that she is temerarious and that all her life has been spent being incontinent in every way; she doesn't look for change. Indurated, so matter-a-factly, till all she knows is suffrage. He is a manqué leader, she is the de-facto ruler, the union is coldly inimical in every way. The order is lost, chaos is the service. And she has shown that she will pugnaciously maintain the "Quotidian" she's established.

In layman's terms, She is predatory.

Let's call her name Mona. Women like Mona have one agenda and one agenda only, to Steal, Kill, and Destroy; be it

Desecration of the Black Man
Empress Makeda Gordon

money, Time, or Energy. The ultimate goal is to acquire what she feels she needs and leave a mess behind when she is done.

These types of women have no regard for the man, any other woman, or the children that may be involved in her game. If it does not serve her purpose, it is a non-factor for her. She runs her "business" like a well-oiled machine. She even has a "Code of Conduct" she operates by.

In this example, I am going to show you the system using Mona. But, keep in mind that Mona represents a collective of women; in some cases the system is emplemented by One woman.

Let's use the example of the five fingers to describe the types of men that she targets.

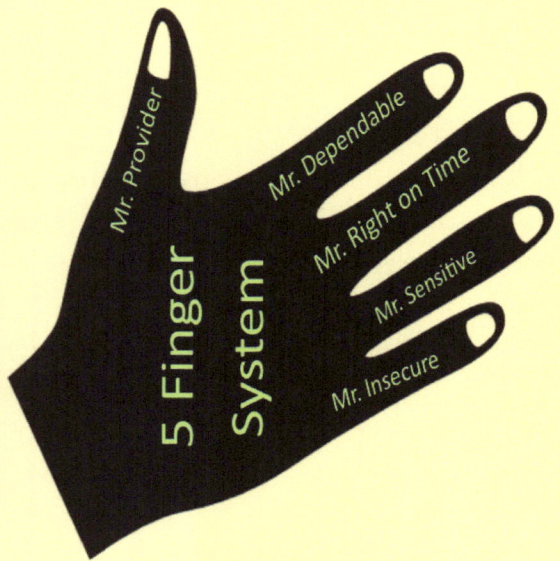

Now that we know what the five types are, let's break each one down.

Desecration of the Black Man
Empress Makeda Gordon

Mr. Provider...

Mr. Provider is the most common type of the five.

Mona decides that she has to replace the guy that was taking care of all of her financial needs, so now it's time to go on the prowl.

When she is looking for money, she makes it her business to "look" like money. So she pulls out her most expensive dress, shoes, pocketbook, etc. She goes to the hair and nail salon and gets all done up. She has a day look and a night look because she doesn't know when or where she will run into him.

It was less than a week since she started her venture when she runs into Jonny. Jonny was a well-dressed, well-educated, tall black man who drove the latest model BMW and smelled like heaven itself. But she is ready! She places herself in his eye view and lingers a bit in that area waiting for him to notice her. Once he does, Game On! He approachs her in the smoothest way a man could. In that moment, Mona turned on and turned up her charm.

The two of them conversed for a bit before exchanging phone numbers. "Locked and Loaded", she thought to herself.

Later that week, Jonny contacts Mona and invites her out for a date. She was so excited. She immediately went out and spent her bill money on a new outfit to impress him. In her mind, she has to always look deserving to the man she is engaging with.

Desecration of the Black Man
Empress Makeda Gordon

They meet up and she is instantly impressed with the evening he had planned for her. All she could think about is how much money he must have. Never once did she give any thought to his personality, respect level, or kindness; all she saw was his generosity.

Fast forwarding to a couple of months down the line, the "dry begging" begins. For those who are not familiar with the term, "dry begging" is when someone just mentions a need without asking for help. Leading up to this part of the game, Mona was sure to maintain her illusion of being sweet, loving, and exotic in bed. She has turned herself into the total package. She listened to everything he has expressed to want and/or need in a woman, and she became THAT.

One evening, after a sexual encounter, Mona turns over and becomes a bit distant. Jonny is concerned because it is outside of her normal behavior. He asked, "what's wrong baby", she replies, "nothing, I just have a lot on my mind". Jonny excepts her answer and simply tells her that he is here for her and if she needs to talk, let him know. The night ended.

Mona stayed M.I.A (missing in action) for the next few days. Sparingly answering Jonny's calls and text messages while staying very short and to the point in all of her responses. Borderline cold. This treatment was not setting well with Jonny, so he decides to stop by her house and have a face to face conversation with her. The bait has now been taken.

Desecration of the Black Man
Empress Makeda Gordon

Jonny arrives at Mona's house that evening and demanded that she tell him what is going on and why she has been so distant. She breaks out into tears. His anger immediately changed into concern. He grabs her and holds her tight, lowers his voice and begs her to share.

Smiling on the inside, Mona spills her guts. She begins to tell him how she is behind on her bills and her job is doing cuts. She went on to say that she really cares about him but has to focus on what she is going to do. Jonny giggles a little, lifts her head and asks, "is that all"? She looks in his eyes and fixes her face to show offense. She responds to him, "That's all? How can you say that? My life is falling apart right now." He replies, Baby, I got you! What do you need?" And just like that, He is now Firmly placed into the position of "Mr. Provider".

His genuine care for her is the Why behind his decision; but to her, she could not care less about his feelings, she just wants the money.

Mr. Dependable

Every woman needs some form of stability and consistency in her life. Even when they are not stable or consistent. The difference between Mona and other women is that her idea of "stability" is "When I call, you come".

Mr. Dependable is generally the long-term fallback guy. He embodies bits and pieces of each type that we will discuss. In most cases, he tends to be the "baby daddy" or "high school sweetheart". We will call his name Marcus for example sake.

Desecration of the Black Man
Empress Makeda Gordon

Marcus and Mona have been in an on again, off again relationship for roughly seven years. They have two children together. Marcus is what most would call a "stand-up" kind of man. He is a loving father and devoted friend. Never runs from his responsibilities and tends to be loyal to people, even to a fault at times.

Meeting at age seventeen, they both matured and changed, which is why they grew apart and ultimately broke up. Mona changed tremendously for the worst, while Marcus grew in the right direction. He had a stable career, home, and mental state. The problem is that he had a soft spot for Mona because of their history, but mostly because of their children. Mona knew this and took advantage of it every chance she got.

Whenever she got lonely, needed money, or just wanted to take off her various mask that she wore, Marcus was who she called. She could be herself with him. What she didn't consider, Ever, was that he was still very much in love with her.

Because they were friends, Marcus knew about Mona's reckless lifestyle, which is why he no longer tries to be in a relationship with her, well, so he thinks.

She has him so attached to her that he cannot even see that he is merely a part of her equation, not a contender for her heart. She gives him just enough time, attention and sex to keep him in position. Meanwhile, he has no clue why he can't maintain a successful relationship outside of her.

Desecration of the Black Man
Empress Makeda Gordon

Knowing the type of man Marcus is, Mona makes sure that she reminds him of how he feels about her at the most opportune times, which is when he is starting to fall for another woman. Losing him completely is not an option. She doesn't mind him dating and being intimate with other women, that leaves her the room she needs to work her plans, but she refuses to allow him to fall in love. She knows that in a relationship, he is honorable and attentive to the needs of his woman, and as an opportunist, she knew that no woman would allow him to maintain the "type" of friendship they had. So she used his heart to block his happiness in order to preserve hers. She even uses the kids when she loses too much ground. She cuts him in and out as it suits her.

Marcus is oblivious to these tactics. Absolutely blind when it comes to Mona. He has convinced himself that she could never treat him the way she does the men she encounters. He just sees her as a young woman having fun, but more importantly, the mother of his children. And she plays that "baby mama" card well.

His integrity is compromised by his self-inflicted obligatory responsibility. He has always been a man that people can count on without hesitation. He has made it his life's purpose.

Marcus has lost some great women along the way, not because he isn't a good man, but because he does not know how to be anything other than Mr. Dependable to Mona, no matter what it cost him. He is incapable of seeing the strings being pulled because he has convinced himself that Not being the "savior" to everyone makes him selfish. He knows no boundaries, so he lives a life of revolving doors. This guy is usually the one with "Mommy issues", and Mona has been around to know this. She has him figured out down to a science. She knows when to call, when to show up, what music to send, what type of sex to give at what time, and how to subtly utilize his children when all else fails.

Mr. Right on Time

Oh, let me start by saying that this man is not worth a darn. He is good for One Thing and one thing alone, SEX. Let's call him Tony.

Tony treats Mona according to her worth. He knows exactly who and what she is, but she is a sure thing anytime of the day or night. He is rude, inattentive, and a true player. He is the male version of Jezebel. He has his own game that he is playing. Still, she can't resist him.

This is the guy that she cooks and cleans for. The one that she asks for nothing from. But whenever he calls, no matter what she is doing, she makes herself available. She will drop everything to get that pounding.

Ironically, Mona gets her feelings hurt with almost every encounter. When they are together, she is the Queen, up until they take care of business, after which, he turns into a familiar stranger. It is almost as if she is trespassing on his property and he wants her to leave.

Desecration of the Black Man
Empress Makeda Gordon

Date night for this "couple" is generally, "Netflix and Chill". He can't risk being seen in public with her, even though she is beautiful and built well. To be seen out together would cramp his style. He needs the liberty to meet new people at his discretion. And she obliges.

Out of all the men that Mona interacts with, no one satisfies her body like Tony does. She locks in on the sex and goes with the flow. After all, all of her other needs are met by the other four men in her circle. And for many women, sex is a direct connection to the heart. The better the sex, the more brain cells they lose.

Never mind the fact that she is treated like a dirty little secret, this is the man that she actually cares about. Imagine that!

The irony of it all is that she believes that if she does enough and is good enough, he will change his ways and choose her; kind of like how the men in her life feel about her.

She never shares with him what she does, nor does he ask. He doesn't care. The fact that he is able to live a life where women are at his beck and call, not only satisfies his ego, but it also authenticates his thoughts of "a woman's worth". She is directly but unconsciously showing him that his theory of women is Truth.

Mr. Sensitive

This man is a sitting duck; an easy target. In most cases, he was raised by a single mom or a female dominated household. So his level of emotionalism is vastly imbalanced against his masculine logic.

"Shane" gives Mona all the tenderness she can stand. He is the reason that she is able to do what she does. He superficially takes care of her "heart". So she is able to be cold hearted toward the rest.

Shane is the guy that whispers all of the sweet nothings in her ear, gives her foot massages and back massages. He strokes her ego; constantly telling her how beautiful she is, how great a woman she is, etc. etc. He makes her feel better about herself. And she loves it. Until….

Mona sucks up all the love and affections that he provides, but she views him as weak. She could never love him. He is too accepting and agreeable. There is no challenge with him. He believes every word out of her mouth and accepts every excuse with an understanding heart.

Sounds good, but it annoys her. This guy is usually the opposite of what her taste in men is, physically. He isn't "ugly" but he is teetering on the fence. He has some confidence but not full confidence in his ability to obtain a woman of her "caliber". He has been so nurtured, really over nurtured, that he thinks and feels as a woman does. He has no experience with the strength of a man. And has no Leadership Qualities.

This is great for Mona because she can effectively play on his sensitivities.

Desecration of the Black Man
Empress Makeda Gordon

She never asks for any money or sex. He frankly is not good at providing either. But he is the one that stays after "love making" and holds her. He listens to her woes attentively. He even cries with her when she is hurting. Sometimes he cries before she does. This is a turn off for Mona.

The only purpose he serves in her life is that of a sounding board. She dumps on him.

Yes, she has sex with him because it is her vice to keeping him around. But she gets no fulfillment from it other than a warm body to cuddle up to after the fact.

Shane falls in love easily and falls hard. He is so in awe of her that he sets a blind eye to her flaws. He knows that he only sees her, or even hears from her a few times a month, but he goes with it. This man is committed and faithful to the "idea" of her.

He stays in a place of hurt feelings when she disappears and becomes the happiest man alive when she returns. She knows this and uses it. He is the closest thing to a relationship as she is going to get at this point. By choice.

Shane is the one man, that when she is with him, she wishes that she could combine all the other attributes from the other men into, to create her perfect guy. Knowing that that is unrealistic, she just taps into him as she needs too.

Mona knows that Shane is crazy about her, she counts on it. When she is with him, she becomes him. She gives him his fill of adoration and phenomenal sex to keep him believing in the possibilities.

She lies to him at every turn to maintain his faith in her. And it works. His heart does not get in the way of her motives because it satisfies what her need of him is. So she strings him along for as long as she can to maintain her corrupted balance.

Mr. Insecure

Poor baby. This guy is not easy on the eyes and he knows it. He usually is older, the "Sugar Daddy" type. The fact that Mona even looked in his direction, let alone considered him, renewed his faith in God (so to speak).

He is very financially comfortable but has let himself go over the years, so he hasn't aged well. His self-esteem has been flushed down the toilet, right along with his pride. Although "Earl", still has plenty to offer by way of personality, he is constantly comparing himself to the men in this new-age "fit life". His memories of the athlete he used to be, blocks his ability to embrace where he is right now. So he has stopped trying. He spends his life now trying to buy the affections of younger women to make himself feel important.

Earl is the type of man that leads with his wallet. Now you may think that he would fit the "Mr. Provider" guy, but he doesn't because he isn't the type Mona wants to be seen with.

Truth is, if Earl was able to embrace his age with grace, he would be the ideal partner for any woman. But his low self-esteem prevents that. So he ends up with a bunch of trophies chipping away at his retirement fund.

Mona ran into Earl at a holiday party that her job had. He was one of the silent partners with her company, so she had never seen him before. But, because of who she is, she is always looking to "upgrade" her current roster; she never goes anywhere without looking like a bag of money and smelling like a bowl of exotic fruit.

Earl spots her across the room almost immediately, but he admires her from afar. Already convinced that she is out of his league, and not realizing that it's the other way around.

As the evening progresses, he works up the courage to say hello, she turns and smiles flirtatiously. What he doesn't know is that she has already gotten all the information about him that she needs. With one look at the Salvatore Ferragamo's on his feet, she knew what his wallet looked like. So she began to ask around to find out who he was and then started her systematic way of getting noticed. She lingered.

Mona and Earl chatted for about a half hour before he blurted out the words, "Come away with me". She giggled, then responded, "Excuse me". Earl replies, "I have a business trip coming up in two weeks to Italy and I was going to go alone, but I'd love it if you would be my guest". She stared in amazement. She did not know this type of money. So she changed the subject, not wanting to seem so easy. He took that as a no.

Desecration of the Black Man
Empress Makeda Gordon

A few drinks later, she says "Ok". At this point he doesn't know what she is responding to, so he asked. She says "ok I'll go with you to Italy". He was so happy but still wanted to know what changed her mind. She responded that he was such a perfect gentleman that she felt she could trust him. She continued on saying that he made her feel comfortable. Well, needless to say, that stroked his ego very well.

And just like that, they were on a plane. The trip was scheduled for five days. Mona played her cards close to the vest. She did not sleep with him until day three. But when she did, man did she pour it on thick.

Not only did she give him the best sex of his life, screwing him nearly to the point of a heart attack, but she faked the infamous "emotional orgasm" at the end. She cried and poured out every compliment she could think of on him. She pulled energy from every man in her infamous "Five". She was adamant about locking this one in for the long haul.

She channeled energy from "Mr. Dependable" by claiming to have never had anyone in her corner that she could count on; she channeled "Mr. Sensitive" by tugging on his heart strings with her tears; she channeled "Mr. Provider" by relaying all of her financial woes and her struggles as a single mother; She took every trick that "Mr. Right" on Time taught her in bed and poured it into him; all to work on his insecurities hard enough to get him to buy into her literally and figuratively. She had to make him believe in her. And it worked!

Desecration of the Black Man
Empress Makeda Gordon

Six months later, they were married. Two years after that, just long enough to qualify for alimony, they were divorced.

Why do you think I used the term, "channeled energy"?

Our every interaction with people is either an exchange of energy, a release of energy, or a drawing of energy. Energy can be time, emotions, or money; anything that has an effect on your livelihood.

Mona, and women like her, are Energy Vampires. Not every woman operates within the full "Five", but most "Jezebels" operate within two or three.

The sole purpose of a Jezebel Woman is to drain a man for all that he has to offer, whatever that may be. She is cold and calculated, self-centered and self-absorbed. Borderline, if not fully, Sociopathic. A Black Widow if you will. Every man she touches, she kills a part of him.

In some cases, she damages his heart, in others she damages his perception of black women; but in every case, he will no longer be the same after her. Even in the case of Mr. Right on Time, he is the one that will never settle down, he will never have to. Why would he buy the cow when he gets all his milk for free?

Desecration of the Black Man
Empress Makeda Gordon

Introducing
Mr. & Mr.(s)

Chapter Seven

You got the ring and the last name that you've been working so hard for. It's your wedding day and nothing or no one can kill your vibe.

The most beautiful wedding, the perfect dress, the love of your life and a promise for forever. What more can a girl ask for? Life is absolutely perfect.

Tammy and Eric have been together for five years and have two children. He is the answer to all of her prayers. She could not be happier. He caters to her needs, tends to the children and carries the bulk of the financial responsibility. Tall, dark and handsome with a sex drive to write home about. But best of all, he only has eyes for her. What is there to possibly complain about. Well, nothing when you are standing in Tammy's shoes. But for Eric, it is a different view.

Don't misunderstand me, Eric loves Tammy with all his heart, but he struggles with being happy in this relationship.

Desecration of the Black Man
Empress Makeda Gordon

Tammy is a twenty-eight-year-old Executive Secretary who is extremely driven. Raised by a strong and independent single mother, she was taught to "never let a man control her". The problem is, she was never taught the difference between Leadership and Control. With this mentality, the only one who suffers is Eric.

A day in the Walker house is not all flowers and candy. Prior to marriage, Tammy was sweet, attentive and very loving; but once that ring hit her finger, all bets were off.

Fast forwarding, three years into the marriage, the tables have turned. Eric's company, where he held an upper management position, downsized and Eric was laid off.

At first, Tammy was totally supportive and stood by her man. But after six months of resumes being submitting to no avail, Tammy began to grow frustrated and, just like that, she changed.

Not a day went by that she did not remind Eric, at some point, that he was worthless. She constantly spoke down to him, even to their family and friends. Never mind the fact that he was trying daily to regain his footing, her perception of her once "knight in shining armor" was altered. How could she go from loving him so deeply to placing him in a category of losers? I'll tell you how; she took the hedge of protection from around them and allowed anyone and everyone in for counsel.

The harder he tried, the tougher she judged him. While looking for work, he would take care of all the cooking and cleaning and would do odd jobs wherever he could find them.

Desecration of the Black Man
Empress Makeda Gordon

just to be able to contribute something to his family. But nothing was good enough for Tammy.

The shift started overnight, literally. Tammy attended a Mother's Day lunch with her family this year. It was supposed to be a celebration of Motherhood, but it took a turn for the worst and turned into a male bashing event. The majority of the women in attendance were either single or unhappy.

Oh how they went on and on about their "no good" men. He's lazy, he's broke, he's a cheater, he's a liar, the list of complaints went on and on.

Now, in her heart, Tammy knew that her husband did not fit ANY of these descriptions that she was hearing. But she did what many women often do, she applied her selective hearing.

If one woman called her man lazy, she would tune out the how, and visualize Eric being asleep on the couch when she gets in from work. If she heard another say that her man was broke, all she could think about was how she was pulling all the financial weight in the house. Even knowing that her sister's husband has not had a single job for the twelve years that they have been together. And to top it all off, Mom cuts in with her, single and never married self, and decides that she is going to give her two cents. Tammy was all ears. After all, she valued her mother's opinion and admired her strength.

She begins to tell the young women that they were foolish. She goes on and on for nearly twenty minutes; just to end it all with…

Desecration of the Black Man
Empress Makeda Gordon

"The problem y'all are having with y'all men is that you have not put your foot down. Y'all just take whatever they want to give. If he not acting right, you ain't acting right. What he won't do, another man will".

What horrible advice coming from an elder woman.

Meanwhile, Tammy is sitting there soaking it all up. And in that moment, she made a decision. She decided to take control of her household.

On top of all of the verbal abuse she was already inflicting on Eric, she began to treat him as a guest in "her" house.

She never recognized or appreciated any of Eric's homemaking efforts, to begin with, but now she has placed an expectation of them on him. If he came to her and said, "baby I fixed that cabinet in the kitchen that was bothering you", her response would be, "Good, it's about time you are making yourself useful around here".

At this time, the only work he could find was freelance landscaping with a friend of his. It didn't pay much but he did bring in some money, and he put every dime into the house.

When she sat down to pay the bills, she would send him away from the table. He would try to fight back, but at this point, he was exhausted with being belittled.

She started hanging out with friends and family more often, leaving him to tend to the kids. And only gave him sex when she deemed him "worthy" or she needed it.

Desecration of the Black Man
Empress Makeda Gordon

His anger grew as his love dwindled. She never even noticed.

She spoke ill of him in front of his friends and belittled him to her family. Everyone in their immediate circle lost respect for him, but only because they were getting one side of the story. Eric was not the type to air his dirty laundry.

Life stayed this way for the next couple of years. The children are getting older and see their father as weak. He is so beaten down, almost unrecognizable to those who knew him best. But he doesn't leave because he wants his marriage to work.

What I didn't mention is the infidelity that has crept into this once solid relationship. Both Tammy and Eric are having affairs and fighting about it constantly. Neither of them cares about the marriage anymore, but no one will walk away.

Tammy fills all the empty spaces with random men, while Eric has been seeing the same woman for the last two years.

He starts spending nights out, cursing at Tammy and calling her all kinds of names. And she reciprocates.

One day in the fall, Eric gets a call from his former employer telling him that they are opening a new office and wants him to manage it. He was ecstatic. He could not wait to tell Tammy the good news. After all, it's been nearly five years since he had what he considered a real job. All he wanted to do was celebrate with his wife. But she was hearing none of it. She simply gave him a fake smile and mumbled: "it's about time".

Desecration of the Black Man
Empress Makeda Gordon

This infuriates Eric. He finally sees that there is NOTHING that he can do that will please his wife. So he decides to go celebrate without her. And that is exactly what he did. He called his mistress and they went out on the town. Eric did not return home that night.

At about noon the next day, Saturday, he walks into the house to a furious wife, screaming and fussing with him. Eric simply walks up the stairs in silence and begins packing his clothes. He tells his wife she can have everything, all he wants is OUT! Her reply to him is "FINE, go!

A few weeks later, Eric called Tammy to request the kids for the weekend. She approves begrudgingly.

That Friday, Eric shows up in his new S500 Mercedes Benz. Tammy saw the car pull into the driveway and got excited. She yelled for the kids and nearly ran to the door; then she abruptly stopped in her tracks. As she approached the end of the porch, she noticed that someone was in the passenger seat. This infuriated Tammy to her core.

Eric steps out of the car, looking like he just stepped out of a magazine and says "hello"; Tammy was stuck. Once she found her voice, she blurted out, "How dare you bring that ***** to our house". Eric chuckled and asked where are the kids? At that moment, the kids came running out excited to see their father. To add insult to Tammy's self-inflicted injury, Rebecca steps out of the car and greets the children.

That's right, Rebecca, aka Becky. She was the woman that Eric had been having a long-term affair with. She was tall,

Desecration of the Black Man
Empress Makeda Gordon

slender, blonde and soft spoken. If you can imagine the look on Tammy's face and the fury working on the inside of her. She summoned Eric to come to the porch, he started to walk in Tammy's direction, when Rebecca gently said, "Baby, that's not what we are here for", and he instantly turned. He told Tammy that he was just there to get the kids and he didn't want any trouble.

You would think with the children present, she would have curbed her tongue, but no, she didn't, not even a little bit. She screamed everything that came into her diluted mind as Eric and Rebecca rushed the children into the car. She called Rebecca everything but a child of God, and Eric likewise.

The happy couple backed up and drove away as if she was not even talking to them.

Tammy could not make it in the house fast enough to tell everybody how Eric was a "sell out".

The infamous "Snow Bunny", Black man's kryptonite, the Black woman's arch enemy. Aren't those some of the terms we use to describe interracial relationships? Wait, correction, Black and White relationships.

While this type of relationship, is not, nor will it ever be my twist; for some people of African descent, it is. It is also true that intermingling between races is a new aged phenomenon, or at least we think.

Desecration of the Black Man
Empress Makeda Gordon

Black women are extremely upset with the number of "brothers" that are "crossing over", but want to take NO responsibility for driving them there. You can only tear someone down for so long before they become bitter and broken toward you and every thing that looks like you.

It is a hard truth to understand how we as Black Women contribute to this "crossover". But in some cases, not all, we do.

The Black Woman does not know or understand her power. Her presence can make or break our counterpart. How we handle their hearts play a big part in "where" they run for safety.

As an Author, I can tell you, without a doubt, that white women are my largest customer base, and I write to and for Women of Color Only. This tells me one thing, They are studying us. They are taking the time to get to know our flaws and the strength in our men, and then they become… Mona! Not always out of spite, but most times because they realize that no man on earth loves harder than the Black Man, and they want that; Every woman wants That!

So, did Tammy run Eric into the arms of the "white woman"? Maybe, maybe not, but what she did do is send him into the wilderness dying and seeking refuge. And that is something that she needs to hold herself accountable for.

Epilogue

There is no question that a man makes his own decisions as an adult. What this writing is conveying is that every action has a reaction.

There is a responsibility and accountability that we must acknowledge as Women, as Wives, as Mothers, and as Sisters, and that is to present ourselves as a valuable individual that not only can be respected but also gleaned from.

Many of my writings present the feminine dynamic in the masculine view. We, as women, are the life givers. That does not end at giving birth; giving life also means contributing to life. The image, interactions, and conduct that we present, as women, shapes, and molds the way boys and men think, feel and treat us; and is also a representation of the future generations of women to come.

Most Black communities are disassembled, meaning, broken families, poverty, crime and overall dysfunctional. However, it has not always been that way. There was a time when we were unified and depended

Desecration of the Black Man
Empress Makeda Gordon

on each other; we worked as a village because all we had was each other.

Now we have this modern day society, this westernized society that has infiltrated our neighborhoods with drugs, limited education, scarce employment opportunities, etc.; completely destroying the core values that we once lived by. But, they did not just send in these seeds of discord, they also molded the minds of our people to become dreamers instead of doers.

The Black Man has always been undeniably the hardest working man since the beginning of time. He was not lazy nor was he dependent. He did not make excuses, he made Magic. He was a Creator, The Creator of All things in this realm.

Even if we were to take into consideration the "ideas" that may have come from the European minds, who do you think put in the labor to bring the idea to fruition, The Black Man. Now trust me I am clear that Black Women carried a heavy burden as well, but when it came to hard labor, it was our men who carried the load.

Fast forwarding back up to today's time, the era of information and technology, a time where we are able to get educated and make a decent living; is it reasonable

Desecration of the Black Man
Empress Makeda Gordon

to say that the aggressive digression of the mental state of the Black Man is solely the fault of oppression? I would have to disagree.

If you take a look at the state of the Black Man, in general, as a whole, we can identify the issues quite easily. To name a few…

- Unemployed/Underemployed
- A Philanderer
- Absent Fathers
- Homosexual/Bisexual
- Abuser

I could go on and on with all the descriptions that are used to identify our Kings, and in some cases, those titles do apply. Notice that I did not mention thugs or criminals, my reasoning is because I believe that the majority of our brothers who are out here committing these crimes are doing so for the reason of provision, it's just unfortunate that there is an entire war ground that comes with it. Not saying that I agree with the criminal path, but I am saying that I understand it. There are no boundaries to what I will do to feed my children, and that goes double for most of our Kings.

So, if we look at the bullet points that I have made, you will be able to connect the dots after reading this book.

Desecration of the Black Man
Empress Makeda Gordon

As a village, we were all interlocked, blood or no blood. We are identified by the color of our skin and the struggle that comes with it. As little as thirty years ago, we still had a remnant of this type of community. Our mothers gave the teachers, anyone on our block, and anyone who watched us as a child, permission to correct us however they saw fit (within reason) according to the wrong they caught us doing. In those days, we were careful in the entire neighborhood, not just on our street, because we knew that word would make it home one way or another Even the average street thug was respectful to the elders. There was a standard, a hierarchy, and a deep regard we conducted ourselves with and put into our children.

But today we have allowed this "westernized/european" way of life to derail us. If you have ever read any of my books, you know that it is my firm belief that it all started with the "Women's Liberation" movement.

Women's Lib was never the Black Woman's battle. Some of the issues that were fought for were issues that would affect us; however, at the time that that movement began, our voices were not even heard. Yet, we took on the white woman's fight against her man to become equal to them. While simultaneously fighting for equality as a race. Somewhere in that mix, we took the rage from our racial injustice and infused it with the feminine equality battle. The lines got crossed tremendously.

But how could they not? We walked onto a battlefield in a strange land, without any weapons, leaving our husbands behind, the ones who vehemently protected us in EVERY battle, and expected to win. How does this concept make sense?

The Black Man has always been deeply feared by the Europeans; simply because they did not understand how he could be so good at Everything with no formal education. They feared what it would mean to educate him. How much more powerful would he become? So they oppressed him the hardest. After they stripped him, emasculated him, and deprived him of learning, they were still so lost as to how his Will was not broken and he kept fighting, and kept moving forward, with Pride.

This was an anomaly to the European. They had to look deeper and find a new mode of operation. They needed to find out what was it about the Black Man that was fortified. How is he still standing? That was when it hit them. It was The Black Woman!

Oh, she was his Rock. After a long day of hard work and kissing butt just to barely feed his family, he would come home and She would be there. Greeting him as if

Desecration of the Black Man
Empress Makeda Gordon

he was the President of the United States. She took the little food and created sustenance for his body, she rubbed his back, encouraged his heart; she showed him appreciation and adoration; she made love to him passionately, taught his children to honor and give him the respect that he was not getting in the free world. She kept his house and his children well. The Black Women gave him a palace to come home to, no matter what the living conditions were. She understood his plight and was determined not to add to it. She allowed him to be the King, the Head, the Cornerstone of his home and family.

Once this truth was realized by the European, something had to be done. So they waged war against the Black Woman! There was no other way into him.

It started with Women's Liberation.

They gave her his jobs, then started taking her to be their "wives"; offering her a "better life". The divide and concur began.

The Europeans presented her with the "other side" of life. They passive aggressively began to brainwash her against her Black Man. The list goes on and on with the tactics that they used. Eventually, they sent their women to target the few Black Men that were becoming successful.

Desecration of the Black Man
Empress Makeda Gordon

How did this affect and continues to affect the Black community? The Black Woman has lost respect for the Black Man because she now sees him as a failure, as not having tried or is trying. Her perception is altered. She sees only power and materialism as a success.

As for the Black Man, he goes through his life struggling to make a good life with his African Queen, but once he makes it, he is presented with a false perception of what success looks like as well. He has been convinced that the last piece to the puzzle is the white woman. He has on blinders. He is unable to see how this battened disregard for the woman who stood by him has caused bitterness.

So now we have a society of Black People who see the opposite sex as lazy, complacent, and failures or as angry, loud, and disrespectful.

Meanwhile, the Black Women is single and worn down from fighting for her "independence". Successful or not, she is tired. She blames her partner, the Black Man, and is bitter against him. So she stays single or crosses over. And the Black Man is either creating every criminal act possible to regain the attention and/or respect of the Black Woman, or he has resigned to being with White women and has completely given up on us.

<u>IT WAS NOT OUR FIGHT!</u>

How did it all really affect us? The movement started in the late 1960's so I decided to do some research on the after effects on the family unit of the two major races.

1969 Divorce rate

- Whites: 2.4% ... 39% is wives filing for divorce
- Blacks 3.5% ... 18% is wives filing for divorce

2015 Divorce rate

- Whites: 41% ... 29% is wives filing for divorce
- Blacks 53% ... 42% is wives filing for divorce

Now I don't know about you, but these numbers are disturbing to me, on both sides. Do you see the vast increase in the divorce rate, but more importantly, Who is filing? 42% of all Black divorces are the Black Woman leaving or filing? There is no wonder why people are afraid to even try marriage at this point. The odds of success seem very slim. I do not know how we can go from a divorce rate of 3.5% to 53%, seeing the timeline and not realize the connection.

The biggest lost through it all is the community. Mission Accomplished!

With all of the success we have gained as a people, the moment we marry outside of our race, we fund the European Agenda. It is much bigger than shopping

Desecration of the Black Man
Empress Makeda Gordon

"white". The inheritance to the Black Millionaire becomes white money because it stays with the spouse. This cycle continues and will continue unless we do some reverse engineering.

The bottom-line is that White Women took their fight to the government while the Black Woman took hers home because she had no voice in government.

IT WAS NOT OUR FIGHT!

BUT WE ARE THE ONES SUFFERING.

Not excusing black men's responsibility to step up and fight for their families at all, but black women also have to accept their responsibility as well.

We have to stop over nurturing our sons, we need to teach them responsibility and critical thinking. We have to stop degrading and demeaning our men, and start building them and encouraging them to their full potential. We have to stop presenting ourselves as sex symbols and start presenting ourselves as women of valor. We have to stop fighting and being competitive with our sisters and learn to love, respect and embrace them.

Desecration of the Black Man
Empress Makeda Gordon

Change cannot come, the standard cannot be raised until we, raise it.

From the beginning of time, there has been and will continue to be Jezebels. They serve a purpose, they are here to test the strength of a man. That is something that we cannot change. But, we do not have to become one by societal pressures. In the heart of the black woman, we are virtuous, we are royals, but we are succumbing to a world that is created for you instead of creating your own world.

There will always be an imbalance between the European and the African people, this we can be sure of, but we all co-exist in this world. Why can't we build a nation within a nation? It is not as if we haven't done it before; and under much worst circumstances, if I might add.

As black men, you have to learn or relearn what responsibility to your family and community means. Your women need you to reclaim your throne.

As black women, you also have to learn and relearn how to embrace, build and support your men. Be his backbone again.

Desecration of the Black Man
Empress Makeda Gordon

We all need to fall in love again. In love with who we are, what we are. We have to get back to the basics. Let go of the anger of slavery, know it, yes, but the most important history for us as a people to learn, and hold on to, is the history that slavery interrupted.

Desecration of the Black Man
Empress Makeda Gordon

The Original

Black Magic

Desecration of the Black Man
Empress Makeda Gordon

Also Available....

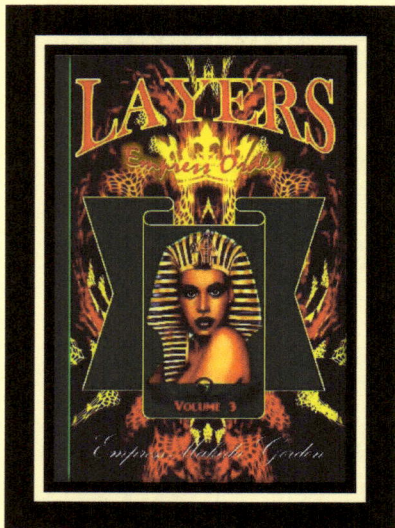

Desecration of the Black Man
Empress Makeda Gordon

Visit us at: Www.sm4publishing.com

Schedule a Seminar: sm4publishing@gmail.com

Follow us on Facebook, Instagram and Twitter: @sm_publishing

Shop Solomon & Makeda Books & Organic Products on our Facebook page

Peace and Blessings!

www.ingramcontent.com/pod-product-compliance
Lightning Source LLC
Chambersburg PA
CBHW042334150426
43194CB00005B/158